Disrupted!

How to Reset
Your Brand & Your Career

Happy Reading Alexandra!
Thanks for helping make this project happen!

Hurst W—

3.30.21

By

Sally Williamson & Hurst Williamson

With Research By LaKesha Edwards

Other Books by:

Sally Williamson & Associates, Inc.

<u>The Hidden Factor: Executive Presence</u>

How to Find It, Keep It, and Leverage It

The shelves are full of books on leadership: how to attract it, how to develop it and how to manage it. But, within the qualities of effective leadership, lies the more elusive concept of executive presence. Some define it as an aura; others say it's a swagger, the ability to command a room. Still others say it's authenticity and personal confidence. And frequently, it's a defining factor in promotions.

<u>The Hidden Factor: Executive Presence</u> validates what executive presence is, how it impacts someone's ability to lead and how to help someone develop it.

<u>Leading Executive Conversations</u>

Be Confident. Be Compelling. Be Concise.

Leading conversations with leaders is a moment of visibility for most seasoned managers. And yet, these conversations can be as much of a liability as an opportunity. And that's because it's hard to determine the right amount of information and define the definitive takeaways. It's the gap between a manager's perspective and a leader's expectations.

This book solves the gap with insights from over 300 leaders who define what they value in communication and how they leverage insights to make decisions. The SW&A structure for executive conversations is a methodology built with a clear message and a flexible framework. And its helped thousands of managers lead dynamic conversations.

Storylines & Storytelling

What They Remember & Repeat

Stories are a universal communication tool because we relate to stories and can see ourselves within the experiences. But, when stories are used in business settings, we expect even more. We expect stories to be remembered and repeated.

It isn't as easy to align stories to business situations and tell stories that are compelling enough to repeat. But we can help you get there. In this book, Sally solves both challenges with concrete tools to shape storylines and stories that deliver impact. It's a three-step formula that leads to compelling communication: a clear storyline, memorable stories and a compelling storyteller.

The book reveals the art and science of storytelling, and the most effective way to shift from a competent communicator to a compelling one.

Published by

Sally Williamson and Associates, Inc.

Atlanta, GA 30305

ISBN 978-0-9837069-2-2

Library of Congress Control Number: 2021901237

DEDICATION

To those who are working through disruption...

...those who've yet to experience it.... and those who've lived it again and again.

...and to the SW&A team, who turned our disruption into an incredible journey.

What Talent Leaders are Saying about *Disrupted!*

"The concept of a 'career' has gotten increasingly complex, and this trend will no doubt continue - if not accelerate - in the coming years. With their characteristic combination of insightful storytelling and practical advice, Sally and Hurst Williamson provide a compelling guide for those who want to proactively and successfully navigate this ever-changing landscape of work. I highly recommend 'Disrupted' for professionals - in any stage of their careers - who want to ensure they have the skills and tools to achieve their career goals in a world where uncertainty, change and 'disruption' are increasingly the norm."

Peter J Wheelan

Former CEO, InsideTrack

Executive Chairman, Roadtrip Nation

"Sally's rationale and approach for intentionally defining personal brand and career development is spot on. As agency has shifted from the employer to the individual for crafting a personal career journey, Sally's framework in Disrupted! provides important and helpful insights to guide and define your career through moments of disruption."

Susan Otto

Chief People Officer

BlackLine

"No one starts their career thinking about disruption, but it happens more frequently than you may think. Knowing how to navigate and reset yourself for the next opportunity is critical. Disrupted! will help you feel prepared and ready to pivot!"

Barbara Blevens

VP, Talent Acquisition

LexisNexis Risk Solutions

"Our partnership with SW&A has had an impact on me and our leaders. Like many others, I've always struggled with presentation skills. SW&A gave me actionable suggestions to develop great habits. As a result, I knew the SW&A team would be ideal for our leaders and we integrated their coaching into our leadership program. SW&A is a great resource for managers and leaders who want to improve their impact."

Jennifer Campbell

Director, Learning & Development

Infoblox

"As a talent leader, I see potential every day; it's actually one of my greatest professional pleasures. And over time, I take note of those that take responsibility for turning potential into opportunity. If you asked me how to do that, I'd give you this book and tell you to follow the insights and guidance that will help you position your brand and share the value of your story. As Sally's book points out, even amidst disruption, you have the ability to dramatically impact your 'next chapter.'"

Scott Murphy

Senior Vice President, Strategic Leadership Development

Boys & Girls Club of America

"SW&A's Disrupted! is an excellent read if you are looking for real solutions on how to navigate through the often unscripted and chaotic transition between defined job roles and undefined job roles where you are expected to just figure it out."

Saviour Anyidoho

Senior Manager, Training and Organizational Development

Zaxby's Franchising, LLC

"Helping our talent reach their full potential is an ongoing challenge in today's fast-paced world. SW&A's clearly laid out approach emphasizes the importance of managing your brand and taking ownership for impressions you leave on others. And, the ability to do that well can make a difference in accelerating or derailing your career path."

Kim Ziprik

Senior Manager, Organizational Development

NASCO

"Sally nicely addresses the topic that continues to arise in every company or industry. You have to take ownership for your career and become personally aware of skill sets required today and expected tomorrow. The ability to position our brand will be the difference in whether you stay ahead of opportunities or watch them pass by."

Ann Clearkin

Head of People Partners (Retired)

Atlassian

"Change is familiar, typically we successfully adjust and pivot, but disruption is change in the form of an earthquake or tornado, erasing paths back to comfort and stability. However, disruption, like change, is full of possibilities. It's the perfect time to rebrand and reconfigure your skillsets for success, now and in the future. Those that don't, will be left behind."

Sharon J Marshall

Executive Succession Manager

UPS

"I love the way Sally explains that you are responsible for your own path. We all must understand our personal brand, know what our skills are and understand how they actually fit in the career we have chosen. Knowing this and believing it, will be the difference between succeeding and not. Vyne's partnership with SW&A has helped me to achieve more than I ever thought possible and has had a successful impact on my career."

Leslie Lyons

Vice President of Human Resources

Vyne

"In today's fast-paced work environment, you'll have many opportunities to shift roles and consider new directions. But you need to be able to present yourself, your brand and your experiences effectively. The SW&A team is a trusted resource to help individuals do that and Disrupted! is a great addition to their approach."

Kim Sullivan

Chief People Officer

Concentrix

Table of Contents

Section I: Disruption

Chapter 1: Disrupted! 1

Chapter 2: Personal Disruption 9

Chapter 3: Corporate Disruption—
Insights from Talent Development 15

Chapter 4: The Perfect Storm 23

Chapter 5: Resets Across Your Career 27

Section II: Resetting Your Personal Brand

Chapter 6: What is Your Personal Brand 37

Chapter 7: Brand Awareness & Feedback 47

Chapter 8: Brand Expectations Across a Career 59

Chapter 9: Presence: Three Key Attributes 65

Chapter 10: Attribute One: Confidence 71

Chapter 11: Attribute Two: Commitment 79

Chapter 12: Attribute Three: Connection 89

Chapter 13: The Virtual Communicator 99

Chapter 14: Building a Brand (Early Career) 109

Chapter 15: Building a Brand (Mid-Career) 123

Chapter 16: Building a Brand (Peak Career) 137

Section III: The Art of the Interview

Chapter 17: Disrupted!...Again   151

Chapter 18: Personal Resets   159

Chapter 19: Corporate Priorities—
Insights from Talent Acquisition   163

Chapter 20: A Step Back or a Step Ahead   171

Chapter 21: Interview Expectations
Across a Career   175

Chapter 22: Resumes vs. Conversations   185

Chapter 23: The Messaging Document   189

Chapter 24: Presence in an Interview   205

Chapter 25: Interviews by Panel   213

Section IV: Building Your Career Narrative

Chapter 26: Your Career Story   227

Chapter 27: Step One: Map Your Journey   235

Chapter 28: Step Two: Define Your Experiences   245

Chapter 29: Step Three: Bring it to Life   257

Chapter 30: Career Stories (Early Career)   271

Chapter 31: Career Stories (Mid-Career)   281

Chapter 32: Career Stories (Peak Career)   293

Chapter 33: Bringing Brand & Stories Together   303

Section I

Disruption

1

Disrupted!

Today is not going to be a good day. You were up half the night worrying. You hardly hear the audiobook you put on in the car to steady your nerves, and as you walk from the parking deck to your office, the cup of coffee in your hand is shaking.

You make it through the front door and past the main lobby. On the way to your desk, you pass your colleagues. Some of them look well-rested as they debate last night's game and swap weekend plans, but others look like you feel. They seem to share your nervous energy, and you get a few knowing half-smiles of camaraderie as you open your email and hope you're wrong.

It's no surprise that half the office seems on edge. Your company was just acquired and, on Monday, your leadership team said the dreaded word that you haven't been able to stop thinking about: "reorganization," commonly referred to as "reorg."

By Wednesday, your manager, Marissa, announced that she was leaving, and last night your new manager, Dan, unexpectedly put some time on your calendar for nine a.m.

today. You worked closely with Marissa for nearly two years, but now Dan has taken over Marissa's team as well as two other teams. You worked on a project with Dan about a year ago, but he's from a different department and most of the work was done remotely. You doubt he really remembers you.

When the clock strikes nine, you walk down to Dan's new office where he is sitting with an HR business partner. He asks you to take a seat and shut the door.

Dan sighs, and you know instantly that you were right.

"Thank you for your work here the last two years," he says. "But the company is moving in a different direction and we don't have a need for your role right now."

The rest of the conversation is awkward and brief, and then you thank Dan for telling you in person as you head back to your desk to pack up your things and wait for a follow-up email from HR.

As you take the long walk from the lobby back to your car, everything starts sinking in. You wonder what you did wrong, how you didn't see this coming months ago, and, worst of all, you worry about what comes next.

Last Friday your world was completely different. You had a plan, you felt secure, but now...you've been disrupted!

Disruption happens to everyone at some point in their careers, and, for many of us, it will happen many times over. Whether you're a new recruit or a twenty-year veteran, a seasoned C-Suite leader or a recent college grad, you can and *will* be disrupted. Favorite managers leave, companies are bought and sold, and boards decide their companies need a new face at the helm. Whether or not you've lived this story firsthand yet, the inevitable truth is that at some point in your career you *will* be disrupted.

In fact, you may even disrupt yourself! We actively seek new roles, go back to school, move our families, or chase dreams. And while that kind of disruption is self-inflicted, it, too, can create lasting impressions that may linger outside of our best intentions.

We take disruption personally. Whether it's a long walk from a desk to a parking lot with our things in a cardboard box or a cross-country move, there's vulnerability that comes with disruption. Even when we're in the driver's seat, we often still feel lost, confused, and a little scared. Yet some people seem to thrive in disruption! Our societal lexicon is full of underdogs who turned failures into successes and went from disrupted dreamers to kings and queens of the hill. So, how do they do it?

Well, as you might have guessed when you picked up this book, there's an art to hitting "reset," and the first step is to understand the shift that's happened in the background of corporate America.

Until recently, the old model for promotions and success within a company had not changed much since the 1950s. You put in your time with a company and the company would slowly bring you along in your professional development, investing in you and moving you along at an established pace to develop new skills and to prepare you for a senior leadership position. But that old and patient model has changed. Companies move at incredible speeds and, as the demand for more specialized and technical skills increases, talent leaders can no longer wait for someone to develop a skill over time. They need the skill right away.

This is why many companies have shifted to a hiring model of "What do we need today?" and "Who can adjust easily to whatever we need tomorrow?"

That's a very different mindset for developing and acquiring talent, and it's a shift that not many employees realize has occurred. Even self-labeled "job-hoppers," who only plan to stay with a company for a year or two, still have expectations that a company will help develop them and advance their career in some way. And while many organizations say they do this, the reality is that most employees do not hit the internal development radar until they meet a specific criterion. That's why, when disruption suddenly hits us, we often feel confused.

- "I didn't know they were looking for that skill set…"
- "I assumed they would teach me any new skills I needed…"
- "I would have learned how to do that if they'd let me know…"

It's rare to see a company continuously grow by hundreds of employees every year. So, when an announcement is made that a company is hiring six hundred new employees, it often means they're moving on from six hundred employees that they already have and hiring six hundred different employees for a new skill set. If this happens to you, it's not necessarily a reflection of the work you've done for the company. You could be meeting or surpassing every metric in your current role, but when a business changes direction, decisions are made fast, and they're clear-cut. Whether you're a front-line employee or a CEO, you either have the skill the company needs…or you don't.

When we choose to disrupt ourselves, we often encounter a similar gap when applying for new roles. Talent acquisition and recruiting teams are constantly trying to fill a variety of needs, often from job descriptions and requests written to describe a specific skill set. And without intention and thought behind how you position yourself, you can be pigeonholed very quickly in an interviewing process.

- "So, Tim, I see you're really more of a sales guy..."
- "Sara, it looks like you've never managed a team this big before..."
- "Darryl, it looks like you're comfortable in a more IT-focused role..."

These are the talent directives behind the disruption each of us will face in our careers. It's ever-changing and, if left to chance, it's a toss-up as to whether you land in the right spot at the right time to be considered for the role you want.

And that's precisely what happened in the story in the opening of this book. Whether you had a plan for your career or not, something happened outside of your control: the company was purchased. To you, it seemed abrupt. You were doing good work and Marissa had even hinted that she wanted you to take over her role when she was promoted next month. To you, all the stars seemed aligned for you to stay at the company, at least for another year or two.

What you didn't see happening prior to Monday was the discussion between your leadership team and the new company's Head of Marketing. Their marketing team felt good about their B2B processes, which you and Marissa had been running at your company for the past two years. They didn't expect to expand their efforts in this area and were actually more interested in your company's recent innovations in your direct-to-consumer strategy. This is part of why they sped up the acquisition process, and it's why they brought in Dan, your company's direct-to-consumer expert, to oversee the newly reorganized team.

Your company has valued what you, Marissa, and the rest of team have accomplished, but now, suddenly, the business' focus has shifted. And what made you so successful over the last year is not a priority for Dan's new team. The new company has a few direct-to-consumer specialists they want to retain, and they're under pressure from the board to keep headcount steady through the merger. Dan's team already has some big expectations attached to them…and he needs specialists to pull them off. This means he doesn't have time to bring people along and teach them the skill set he needs. He needs them to have it now.

This scenario, in various forms, happens every day. People are disrupted, and many are left wondering how they'll ever get through the disruption.

But, as I mentioned earlier, some people thrive in disruption. Or at least, they seem to. So, what's their secret?

Well, the answer is two-part, and it's one we've discovered after coaching our clients for 40+ years and conducting an in-depth survey with hundreds of talent development and talent acquisitions leaders.

Those who thrive in disruption understand two things that will most impact their ability to navigate disruption and reset their careers: **they know how to position their brands** and **they know how to tell their own stories.**

In this book, we'll discuss both, and teach you the art of hitting reset. You'll learn the expectations and road map of brand across your career, and we'll show you how to map your unique career journey and leverage your experiences.

Disruption happens to all of us, but managing it and changing it are real and obtainable skill sets, because resetting your brand and your career starts with you.

Across this book, talent leaders will tell you the very skills they look for across an organization. The only catch? They are skills they'll expect you to develop on your own.

2

Personal Disruption

Disruption takes many forms across a career. Before we begin to solve for it, it's worth first exploring the causes of disruption in more depth. The story we told you in the previous chapter is true, but so are thousands of other stories of disruption, each with their own unique causes and reasons. And while we could fill an entire series of books with these distinctive stories, there are some common themes within disruption to address.

Disruption is not a one-way street. While you can, and most likely will, be disrupted by a boss or a company pivot at some point, we also do things to disrupt ourselves. And what we do, how we do it, why we do it, and when we do it begins to shape the impressions and experiences we'll carry with us across our careers.

In many ways, the first kind of disruption you will face in your career is what you do to yourself.

What We Do

We leave. Plain and simple. "Job-hopping" is a career trend that is often misunderstood and attributed strictly to young professionals. The average person will hold approximately twelve different jobs throughout their career. And while roughly half of that churn will occur in your first decade of employment, this is not a new trend that suddenly appeared overnight with the arrival of Gen Y and Gen Z in the workplace.

What has changed, however, is a more noticeable intent behind what's driving career moves. Among young professionals and other generations, employees today are more self-driven and experimental in their careers than previous generations. The "gig economy" continues to innovate and expand new industries and ways of working, and our employee mindset has adjusted to match that cultural shift.

We're okay with moving companies, changing roles, and starting over. In fact, many of us welcome it (as long as we're in the driver's seat)! We want to be leaders, and we want to start our own companies or be at the cutting edge of new technologies or ideas. And while over the last few years there has only been a slight increase in the average number of job changes an individual will have, this shift in mindset cannot be overlooked. It has removed many of the negative stereotypes of the "job-hopper," and most career coaches will even encourage you to change jobs often to diversify your experiences, increase your salary, and secure promotions.

So, what does this mean? Well, while companies are moving quickly, so are we.

How We Do It

Virtually. When we started writing this book, the COVID-19 pandemic hit the world hard. And while it certainly brought a good deal of disruption to companies and teams, it didn't cause the shift to virtual working by itself. This was already an emerging trend in the workplace and most companies had at least begun to experiment with *some* kind of remote working for their employees.

Prior to the pandemic, close to 10% of employees were working remotely at least one day a week. The pandemic's accelerated push will likely change the way many employees work for the foreseeable future. And as the dust settles and job functions and managers' expectations are realigned toward a virtual or partially virtual work environment, this will no doubt accelerate self-disruption.

Team huddles may shift to Zoom, conferences may stay virtual for a few years, and the option to be a sales manager in Austin covering the Pacific Northwest and reporting to a VP in New York may become more widespread. Shifting the way we work is a form of disruption, and it too will play a part in how we are perceived across an organization.

Why We Do It

We chase ideas. Marketing today has gone beyond just brand recognition. The most successful brands are not just ones who have the best products, but the ones who best align their values and their voices to those of the consumer. We want to work the same way we shop. We want to work for companies who are authentic, who stand for something, and whose stories are relatable.

As we continue to evolve in who we are, we not only chase the things that resonate with us, but also those that excite and drive us.

- "They aren't just shoes…they're a lifestyle choice."
- "It's not just a tea company…it's a commitment to a healthier, greener Earth."
- "We're not just building smarter data…we're changing the way people experience healthcare."

These are the kinds of missions that we are drawn to, and the connections we form with the brands are deeper than you might think. For employees, choosing a workplace is more than just chasing a few logos to add to a resume. Everyone understands wanting to work for the big tech firm or the shiny new start-up on the block, but beyond that, there's a genuine shift among the workforce that values a deeper engagement based on transparency, honesty, and identity. And we're even willing to chase things, to some extent, beyond the old constrictions of salary, location, and industry.

Brand loyalty is something that companies have to earn from their employees, just like they earn it with their customers. And if it isn't earned, we're willing to disrupt ourselves to follow the brands we love.

When We Do It

All the time! Our lives are an ever-changing swirl of difficult decisions and opportunities to hit reset. We may:

- Move our families to follow a spouse's job…
- Go back to school to peruse a different career and get a fresh start…
- Start a family and adjust the amount of time we want to work…

12

These are all decisions that are a natural part of life, and they are also self-imposed disruptions. In general, companies today are more generous in terms of work-life balance than ever before. And while your experience with perks like maternity/paternity leave, remote working, and extended leave might differ, company policies, as a whole, have shifted toward a more supportive attitude regarding their employees' life moments.

The gap, however, is the difference between a company being supportive vs. including you (and your disruption) in their talent planning. While your job might be waiting for you after you return from leave, or stay with you as you move cross-country, that kind of disruption does take you out of the immediate eye of the business. And often, you might return to a new boss, a redefined role, or a much larger team. Even though you took yourself out of the flow with the best of intentions, when you rejoin the team, it won't be the same as when you left.

These examples of "self-imposed" disruption show how many twists and turns we make ourselves before we even consider a company's disruptions and priorities. Our lives change, our families grow, and where we planned to be in five years can shift drastically six months later.

Maybe you've previously considered these to be life choices instead of career disruption. It's true that everything we described was a choice. The challenge is that companies are no longer moving slowly enough for you to step in and out or back and forth around those choices. Because while you're planning for a little disruption in your career choices, most companies are making disruptive choices of their own.

3

Corporate Disruption–
Insights from Talent Development

In our world of communication coaching, we talk to a *lot* of talent development and talent management leaders. One conversation with a new client was particularly revealing. We were designing a coaching program for some of the company's future leaders, and she shared the difficulty of finding and retaining top talent for the company.

"I know that when I onboard a great resource, I only have them for about two years. While it'd be great to build out a series of development steps for a young leader, it doesn't make sense when I know half of them won't be here by the end of it. So, my perspective has shifted to, 'what will you contribute while you're here and what can I do to make you more effective for the company?'"

That's a real dilemma for a talent leader and you can see from her quote that, even with the best of intentions, she can't make a development plan work for everybody. Talent strategies have pivoted from a concentrated, long-term strategy of developing leaders over time, to addressing business needs and standing up new leaders quickly.

We've seen the shift and heard the dilemma anecdotally. But as we began thinking through disruption, we wanted to quantify the corporate perspective more formally. Through a comprehensive survey and follow-up interviews with nearly three hundred talent development and talent acquisition leaders, we found our assumptions matched their insights (see Appendix for full results).

Talent leaders are being stretched to anticipate skills, not just solve for gaps. And company priorities and strategies are shifting at a rate that's hard to stay ahead of. In fact, 47% of our survey respondents said that one of their biggest challenges is that their company's current talent capabilities do not align with the company's future needs. That's a pretty sizable gap! It means that talent teams are looking at either retraining or rehiring nearly half of their workforce. And even with the best of intentions, retraining half a workforce just isn't feasible as a long-term strategy. It's expensive, it slows down a company's operations, and, perhaps most importantly in today's market, it takes too much time.

So, if talent is at such a premium in companies, then where are talent leaders investing their time, energy, and funds? Well, they're investing in two places with very different approaches: first-level managers and emerging leaders (seasoned directors/VPs and above).

Skilled front-line managers are needed to help an organization achieve its goals. Whether you're in sales, marketing, engineering, finance, operations, etc., the first-line manager has a lot of visibility to both employees and customers, and they need to have a specific set of skills to manage the expectations of the brand and of the consumer. Training and support for this group is primarily focused on "hard skills" and whatever technical or specialist skill sets are needed to drive the immediate projects and strategies of a business. While there's a lot of churn at this level of an organization, it still remains a priority for talent teams, so much so that this group was rated the highest training priority across our survey.

The second priority for talent teams are their emerging leaders (Senior Director/VP and up). Interestingly, this group requires the complete opposite training approach. Instead of delivering outcomes of a brand for a customer, future leaders *become* the expectations of the brand. And often, that means a lot more visibility in high-stakes environments. So, training for this group is focused on "soft skills" and whatever communication and leadership traits a talent team can help a rising leader develop quickly.

And as you've probably noticed, there are a *lot* of roles that this approach leaves out. If you don't fall into one of those two camps, you're not alone. And if your own development goals fall outside the scope of what the business needs, there's a good chance you won't wind up on a talent team's radar.

Here's why:

82% of talent development priorities are based on company goals, identified skill gaps for specific tasks, and job roles and functions. And only 8% of talent development programs, initiatives, and events are based on employee feedback and development interests. Talent development leaders told us that employees ask for leadership development, communication, and technical skill development through internal surveys and performance reviews. Yet those desires aren't always in line with their companies' priorities and development investments.

For instance, if you are an individual contributor, you are the lowest priority for talent development opportunities. It is assumed that you will learn new skills from your immediate manager. If you are a first-level manager, you may not receive leadership development unless your role is directly connected to new business objectives, goals, or initiatives. Organizations focus on skill development for jobs needed to achieve their business goals.

When we evaluated spend by departments and function areas, we found that talent development teams tend to focus on targeted groups for broader skills such as leadership, communication, and influence. Specific skills are within department budgets and at the direction of leaders within those divisions. The talent development budgets are heavily weighted toward the two priorities above: first-level managers and leaders.

And as you may have experienced, there are no requirements or guidelines for how leaders spend/allocate or leverage their training dollars. Some invest wisely to keep skills up to date; others see training as an unnecessary expense and a cost that they can keep down within their overall P&L. And in many cases, it's just not a top priority as they look across division goals and expectations.

So, you can see how many employees fall between the cracks by missing training within their function area or not fitting the profile of the talent strategy in a given year. In addition, talent development leaders say that employees have unrealistic expectations and some blind spots about career advancement.

What are some blind spots employees have when it comes to career advancement?

"Thinking career advancement should be quick and that their current competence means they will be successful at the next level."

"Employees think it is the organization or their manager's responsibility to advance them rather than seeing that this is their career, and they need to manage it themselves."

"They do not know what is required to go from point A to point B in their career. And they overestimate their current state."

"Often employees believe that they only need technical skills. This is why we teach them communication skills, which are vitally important for success."

"Employees assume that length of service in a role equals the opportunity to advance."

And when we asked for their reaction to the following statements, they were in unanimous agreement that these beliefs exist in their organizations.

- *An individual should understand their personal brand, know their skills, and understand how they fit in their career.*

- *An individual is responsible for self-managing their own career and development.*

- *An individual must position his or herself for career advancement and promotion opportunities.*

These insights summed up our hypothesis, which is that in today's corporate environment, you need to take ownership for your own development and career advancement. Based on your choices that disrupt career steps as well as companies' priorities that disrupt career steps, there's a lot of room to fall through the cracks. It's safe to say that a company will develop your skills when you're in a role that requires them. But ironically, it usually takes those skills to advance into the role in the first place.

So, whether you stay at one company to advance or move around to a number of different companies, you're going to have to take ownership of your own development.

4

The Perfect Storm

The last two chapters showed you the two perspectives that are changing professional development – disruption caused by personal choices and employer priorities – which have created a perfect storm across many careers.

There is no longer a "tried and true" curriculum for professional development. How could there be? We often move and shift ourselves even before companies move and shift us. A company's ability to develop a leader is driven by timing and priorities. Your ability to develop yourself is focused on personal interests and professional desires. And it's a risky bet to assume that those things will align perfectly with a company's priorities based on the insights we've shared. That's why we're confident that disruption will happen to you.

And that's okay. In fact, disruption will often be something that you choose. But the constant change and acceleration may find you at a point in your career where you don't have a full toolkit of skills – or, from our experience, where you don't have the skills required to reposition and repackage yourself to keep moving ahead.

Here's the good news. Both talent development and talent acquisition agree on what kind of people they look for to fill roles.

Talent Acquisition vs. Talent Development
Top Critical Skills

TALENT ACQUISITION	TALENT DEVELOPMENT
1 Problem-solving & Critical Thinking	1 Communication & Influence
2 Collaborative & Cooperative	2 Agility During Change & Uncertainty
3 Communication & Influence	3 Problem-solving & Critical Thinking

Across industries and across the different levels of an organization, these are the skill sets that will get you in the door (with talent acquisition), keep you there (with talent development), and better position you for advancement opportunities (with management).

Employees who have the ability to communicate to influence, to adapt to changes, and to solve problems are in high demand. And our conversations with survey participants confirmed this! But it will be on you to develop these skills and communicate their impact.

There has never been a better time to define your own career narrative. And there has never been a time when you will be so responsible for trade-offs and outcomes. Disruption is only a challenge if you aren't well-skilled at the reset button.

And to reset, you need to understand two concepts that we've used to help thousands of people reset, redirect, realign, recover, and refocus their career journeys. You need to know how to **represent or present your personal brand** and **how you talk about yourself,** which are the two big development tools outlined in this book. But to understand our tools for reset, we need to first consider where you may be on your career path.

5

Resets Across Your Career

As we set up the theme of this book, we thought about disruption and its impact on a career at many different points on a career road map. Disruption doesn't focus on a single point in a career; it can happen multiple times and at multiple points. And that's why we think the core principles of the book will apply to every point in a career, whether you're in the early stages or the final ones. But the added value you'll find throughout the following chapters will come in the form of shared experiences from our coaching engagements: people we've met and worked with who have dealt with many types of disruption.

We'll share stories of some of the greatest challenges, misconceptions, and blind spots we've seen clients make at different points in their career. Whether you're just starting out or in the "final" phase of your career, it's our hope that these examples and our guidance will help you understand how perspectives shift and challenges evolve over your professional lifetime.

And while the tools are consistent, the demands on a brand for someone a few years out of school are drastically different than those for a C-Suite veteran. Roles are different, audiences vary, and expectations shift. So we'll distinguish between the tracks of a career in terms of expectations and experiences, and we'll share our insights across three unique phases of a career.

Early Career, Mid-Career, and Peak Career

We'll refer to these phases in terms of someone's tenure and their experience. From our perspective, a career phase is really a combination of both. Our career map is meant to help you identify where you are in your own career in order to consider expectations.

Early Career

An early career covers a lot of fast-paced changes. It runs from your first day on the job to the point where you begin to consistently manage others. On average, most people's early career phase lasts a decade. In most roles, you are an individual contributor working as an analyst, specialist, representative, or associate.

Early-career employees enter the workforce eager to make an impact with technical skills. And you can in short order! As an early-career employee, you gain visibility quickly. Credibility comes more slowly. This is the time to build an impression of confidence and trust as a valued employee.

It's critical to develop good habits that will help you pivot and flex whenever disruption occurs. We coach early-career employees to consider two concepts that best support their career advancement in today's shifting environments: visibility and value.

VISIBILITY

The number of managers most employees have in the first decade of their career has continued to climb. On average, most employees have had seven different managers at the end of ten years, which means having a new boss roughly every eighteen months. So, the pattern of a single manager promoting you within a company and creating your next opportunity isn't very reliable.

You'll need to learn how to build relationships and create visibility for yourself. You should begin to build your unique network within a company so that your success is lined up to multiple people and not behind one manager.

VALUE

Focus more on what you can do for a company rather than what a company should be doing for you. Once a company sees value in an employee, they become extremely loyal. But it's the company's perspective that measures values, not your perspective. Raise your hand often; go the extra mile. And don't worry about getting credit every time. Play for the team. Collaborating well with others gets noticed early in a career.

Gaining visibility and adding value to a conversation only matters if you're willing to work hard to deliver on a result. You have to put in the hours to achieve the results. That part of the career journey hasn't changed. Early-career employees always ask, "How long does it take to add value?" And the answer is longer than you think. It takes multiple "at bats" for people to notice and trust in what you can add to a company.

This is one reason why early-career employees get impatient and move from company to company. Be intentional about moving to avoid spinning or always starting over at this phase of your career. Make sure that a new role provides a new opportunity to lead, to gain a new skill set, or to develop a more specific expertise.

Mid-Career

The next phase of a career is mid-career. It's perhaps the longest stretch of most journeys. That makes it the trickiest to define.

Some people advance in their careers through experience and expertise; others advance by expanding responsibility and taking on bigger roles. We think about mid-career as a track someone may stay in for a decade or for the duration of their career. Either way, the first phase of management drives a significant shift in perspective and expectations. The focus of your brand shifts from you as an individual to you as a manager. You're measured on how well you can influence and motivate others. And your brand becomes aligned with your group and your team.

While strategies and directives will come from senior leaders, it is the mid-career managers who are responsible for implementation of new initiatives and products. And in order to drive success with employees, it's as much about how well you listen as it is about what you say. Many mid-career professionals learn this the hard way. They have a few misfires on a bigger stage, and they have to quickly learn the power of impressions and the risks of assumptions.

We coach mid-career managers to consider two concepts to best support their career advancement: clarity and influence.

CLARITY

At the midpoint of your career, you need to focus on how you organize your thoughts. You will have a lot of visibility and access to leaders. Overnight, your ability to represent ideas effectively will impact your brand. You need to learn to add value to a conversation and communicate in a way that connects your idea to a broader business need or opportunity. The ability to make a point clearly distinguishes one manager from another and is often the leading factor for increased responsibility and visibility.

INFLUENCE

As you share ideas, you need to be able to get others on board with those ideas. It's a shift from talking *at* people to talking *with* people. Influence was a top skill called out by talent development and talent acquisition professionals in our survey. It expands your communication skills to think about how you listen, how you connect, and how you ultimately galvanize energy and effort in others.

At the mid-career level, your visibility grows significantly. But along with that visibility comes a responsibility to lead and develop a team. Overnight, you're expected to become a manager, a coach, and a teacher all in one. And those who can will become their organizations' next senior leaders.

Peak Career

When we think about the peak career phase, we're referring to someone who has a lot of responsibility and visibility within a company. "Peak career" refers to a senior leader or a high-visibility leader who has gained influence over decisions and groups. We call it "peak career" because it's the point at which someone has taken on even more responsibility and is valued within an organization because of it. This is the "high risk, high reward" career phase because expectations have reached their pinnacle. It's no longer good enough just to be competent...now, you have to be compelling.

In your peak career, everything has gotten bigger. The size of the team(s) you manage, the number of initiatives you drive across an organization, and your exposure to media, board rooms, and the industry as a whole have all grown in size. And with the increase in responsibility comes an increase in expectations from your employees. They want to know more than what you need from them; they want to know why it matters and where the organization is headed. You represent the brand for the entire company, and, from you, your employees will set expectations for their future, their role, and their next steps. Peak-career leaders can singlehandedly set the tone and emotion that gets an employee group involved and invested in ideas and actions. We coach peak-career leaders to consider two concepts for impact: authenticity and repeatability.

AUTHENTICITY

Authenticity is often associated with honesty, and honesty becomes a very hard expectation to deliver because top leaders think about it as information. But that isn't what most people set as an expectation of leaders! Authenticity is about how you communicate. It means being open and direct in what you can share and positioning yourself as someone they can believe and trust.

REPEATABILITY

Because top leadership roles have the visibility to set tone and emotion, leaders themselves have to bring the capability to do that well. Messaging has to be memorable and repeatable across an organization in order to keep employees informed, aligned, and motivated about what they do every day.

At a peak-career level, leaders take on enormous responsibility for keeping their personal brand and the company's brand well-aligned. Most days, they speak on behalf of employees and they have to stay very close to feedback and input that validates that they understand that perspective and are well-aligned to it.

So, let's look at how brands are established in a work environment and how they evolve and reset across a career.

Section II

Resetting Your Personal Brand

6

What Is Your Personal Brand

Your brand is how people think about you – and talk about you – when you're not around. Think about that for A moment. *It's what people think and say about you, usually when you're not around.* It's how they sum up impressions and share those impressions with others. It sounds intimidating and even judgmental, but we do it all the time.

The impact of those impressions is usually described as an "observation" or an "assumption." And there's a big difference! Consider a scenario in your life, something as simple as new neighbors moving in.

You and your spouse get new neighbors, Ned and Maude. You've been out of town for the last few days, so you haven't had a chance to meet them, but your spouse has. And when you come home, what's one of the first things you'll talk about? The new neighbors! And, when you say, "So tell me about the new neighbors," your spouse may say:

"Well...they're both tall...Ned wears glasses...Maude has red hair...and they moved in on Tuesday morning."
Those are observations from your spouse. Literal truths and certainties because he/she saw them directly. There are no

extrapolations in what they're saying, only established and irrefutable facts.

But is that all that your spouse is likely to share? Of course not! They are likely to add an impression such as:

> "They seem really nice!" or "They seem pretty weird."
> "I think Ned's a musician!" or "Maude doesn't seem like much fun."
> "We're going to love having them next door!" or "I can't believe we got stuck with them."

These are assumptions, and we make them daily, whether we mean to or not. In this case, your spouse is making assumptions and forming personal impressions and opinions of Ned and Maude based off a ten-minute conversation across your fence. Ned might just keep his grandfather's guitar as a decoration and not be able to play a single note. Maude might be feeling overwhelmed by the move or tired from long nights with a new baby. But notice how natural the assumption statements seem compared to the factual observations. That's because, as human beings, we rarely stop at mere observations in our personal lives or at work.

So, let's consider how assumptions impact your brand at work.

Here's another scenario.

Your team gets a new engineer, Jenni, who started on Monday. You were involved in a customer conference for three days, so you haven't met Jenni. But your coworkers have. And when you ask about Jenni, what do you think they will say?

> "Well, she went to Brown…came from ABC Semiconductors….knows Agile really well."

They might start off with something like that. But more likely:

> "She seems great!" or "She's a little greener than I thought we were hiring."
> "She's pretty type A!" or "She's a little shy."
> "We're lucky to have her!" or "I don't think she's a great fit."

These are initial impressions and assumptions, and you'd be surprised how quickly they form and how long people hold on to them. In this scenario, imagine you don't work on a project with Jenni for three months. Then your boss asks you to put together a select group to work on a big project. You can pick anyone you want from the team, and you sit down with your manager to go over candidates. When he says, "What about Jenni?" what will you say? Chances are that you'll base your impression off of what your coworkers told you.

If they told you she seemed great, you'll probably add her to the team as an opportunity to get to know her. But if they thought she seemed "too green," you might pass her over for this opportunity. Jenni might be a brilliant engineer, and the coworker who told you she wasn't experienced enough may have changed their mind. But you got an initial impression in your mind that was based on a secondhand assumption, and it's still there as your only point of reference.

This happens in offices all the time. Impressions formed years ago can come back to stall or impede a career. You didn't do anything intentionally, and you may have been a phenomenal contributor since then, but remember, your personal brand is how *others* perceive and experience you. And the only way to manage those impressions and assumptions that people make about you is to be aware of the brand you put forward and be a little more intentional about how people experience your brand.

In our brand workshops, we start by asking participants to create a brand profile. The illustration below highlights how we capture this.

MY PERSONAL BRAND

Your brand is like a trademark that combines all the elements of you into someone else's experience of you.

PART I: Impressions – What You Think
List six attributes that you believe best describe you.

1. _____   4. _____
2. _____   5. _____
3. _____   6. _____

PART II: Impressions – What Others Think
List attributes that you think others would describe of you next to each statement.

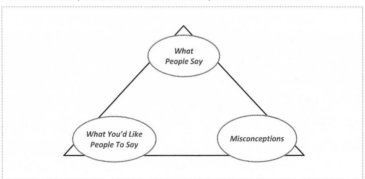

First, we want to know how an individual would describe their own brand, the attributes that they think best describe who they are, and the attributes they value in themselves. So, let's take a closer look at Jenni from the example above.

Below, you see that she described herself as:

**Compassionate, Earnest, Honest,
A Team Player, and Shy**

It may surprise you to know that most people haven't really thought about this. They don't want to think about the core attributes of their brand until they're asked about them. Maybe you feel the same way. So, here's the first takeaway: if you aren't sure of the core attributes of your brand, then there's a pretty good chance they don't come through as consistent impressions. Or if you define your brand in terms of what others have told you, then you're letting others shape impressions rather than owning them yourself. And that's the second part of the exercise.

We use the triangle illustrated below to capture the impressions others have of you, from your perspective. The top of the triangle represents things people say about you most often. These are attributes that people say so often that they've actually shared them with you.

In our example, Jenni often hears people describe her as:

Kind, Reliable, and Quiet

The bottom left of the triangle represents things you wish people said more often. These are attributes that are important to you, but you don't think they get noticed often.

Jenni's triangle says:

Compassionate, Knowledgeable, and Strategic

So, we're learning that Jenni is often recognized for being kind, but she wants to be seen as knowledgeable as well. This seems to matter to her.

And the bottom right of the triangle represents things you think are misconceptions about your brand. These may be initial impressions that you haven't been able to leave behind or feedback you've gotten that you disagree with.

For Jenni, it's when people think of her as:

A Pushover, Reserved, Tentative, and Unsure

You can see a theme developing. Jenni is quiet and shy. Others read that as tentative and think she's often unsure of herself or her thoughts. She wants to be seen as knowledgeable and, in order to illustrate that attribute, she's going to have to speak up and not stay quiet in meetings.

Here's what Jenni's complete brand map would look like:

Your brand is like a trademark that combines all the elements of you into someone else's experience of you.

PART I: Impressions – What You Think

List six attributes that you believe best describe you.

1. Compassionate   4. Earnest

2. Team Player   5. Honest

3. Intelligent   6. Shy

PART II: Impressions – What Others Think

List attributes that you think others would note about you next to each statement.

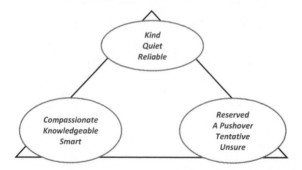

Once you have a clear picture of your brand, then we talk to you about intentional choices. We don't actually try to change your brand; you define what you value and the attributes that represent you in your self-impression. Your brand is like a trademark. But, as you can see from the example, not all attributes come through consistently. And that's where we can improve your impact.

We think about how people experience you and how those impressions take shape. They form impressions in meetings, hallway chats, presentations, and project teams. And over time, those experiences shape impressions.

- I might perceive someone who continues typing an email while I'm talking to them as rude or not valuing my opinion or time
- I might perceive someone who talks over coworkers in meetings to make a point as a know-it-all or a bully
- I might perceive someone who sends short, four-word emails as curt or impatient.

Your personal brand evolves as people form initial impressions and then get to know you better. Think back to the team your boss asked you to put together. Those initial impressions from Jenni's first week might aid her or prevent her from having a great opportunity three months later. That's an example of the weight of a coworker's impression. The stakes get higher as impressions are set with leaders who experience your brand less often, or for leaders with employees who only experience their brand in large settings.

We know that impressions are important and long-lasting, but the question becomes, what should you do about them? It comes down to awareness and intention. Over the next few chapters, we'll explore how to raise your own awareness of impressions by seeking feedback, and then go over intentional choices that can influence these impressions.

The foundational skills we'll teach you in the following chapters are the same for everyone. But they'll become uniquely yours as you consider how to deliver on the attributes you want others to experience in your brand. And as you consider how you want to be perceived, think back to Chapter 3 and the critical skills that talent teams are looking for: someone with strong communication and influence, the agility to flex and change during times of uncertainty, and the ability to think critically and solve problems. Are these already attributes of your brand, or things you need to develop further or illustrate differently?

The starting point for anyone is to gain a clear understanding of how your brand is perceived today and then to consider where you'd like to strengthen it. Then, you can use the next chapters to help you get there.

7

Brand Awareness & Feedback

We recently worked with a client, Hugh, who started with a new company amidst a little chaos. In his first month, his division underwent a reorg and he was left without a job description for three months. He attended what he described as "a slew of confusing and poorly organized strategy meetings" every week with upper management, always seated in the back and never given an opportunity to participate in the discussions.

Sometimes their Chief Operating Officer, Cindy, would attend these meetings, but that seemed to only bring additional people and confusion to the meetings. Hugh admits he kept his head down, often engaging more with his phone than the room.

Fast-forward another six months, and Hugh's engagement improved. He was placed in a new role after the position he'd originally been hired for was eliminated. The new role gave him a clearer picture of the day-to-day operations of the company and how his role supported tangible business outcomes. Hugh was doing well in this role and was up for a promotion at the beginning of the new year. He had a good working relationship with his immediate manager, who was on the promotion committee and mentioned on multiple occasions that he thought Hugh was a shoo-in for a promotion.

…Which is why the feedback Hugh received during his end of the year review was so shocking. A week before he expected to be promoted, Hugh met with his manager and his manager's boss for his review and was told that he would not be promoted in the coming year. Hugh was stunned, but after a moment he asked for feedback. He was doing good work, and he thought he had made some real contributions to his new division over the last six months.

Hugh's manager was quiet and, after some additional prodding, it was his manager's boss who finally gave Hugh some tough feedback.

"You seem disinterested here," she told him. "I didn't see you take an interest in the strategy meetings during the reorg, and neither did Cindy. The promotion involves a lot of cross-divisional collaboration, and it doesn't seem like a good fit for you right now."

Without realizing it, Hugh had created a negative brand for himself in his first three months at the company. It might've seemed like the leaders weren't paying attention to him, but they were. And you heard the impressions they formed: "disinterested and not a good fit for a cross-divisional role." Once Hugh rotated out of his first role, he did not have another meeting with Cindy or his current boss's boss, so they held on to the last impression of him from his early months at the company.

In this case, it didn't matter that Hugh had made great strides in his current role or that he had a good relationship with his immediate boss. When his name came up for the promotion, a negative brand held him back.

Hugh's experience isn't that unique. Impressions are set easily, and sometimes they last longer than we realize, especially with people who don't experience us often. In Hugh's case, his leaders held on to an initial bad impression and used it as the basis for deciding not to promote him.

What would have been different if Hugh had known about those impressions? We'd like to think he would have been able to change those impressions and move ahead with the promotion. In Hugh's case, he had no idea he had created a bad impression, so his manager's feedback came as a difficult surprise.

Not everyone likes to receive feedback. And few managers like to give it.

When we ask managers to share their most challenging communication situations, "feedback" always makes the top three. People managers don't like giving it, they often feel that they aren't good at it, and they don't always know how to move an employee beyond it.

And yet, when you ask people about pivotal moments in their careers, they reflect on feedback or direction that set them on a different course or got them over a hurdle. They may not have liked "the gift" of feedback when it was received, but they valued the impact it had on helping them move forward.

It doesn't get easier to receive feedback as a career advances. In fact, it gets harder for a leader to ask for it and certainly harder for colleagues to give it. You have to make the decision to ask for feedback frequently and to welcome it so that colleagues feel good about giving it.

Let's look at asking for feedback, reacting to feedback, and managing through the feedback you get.

Asking for Feedback

Asking for feedback is the most direct way to understand perceptions around your brand and impressions shared about you across a department or organization.

But be careful.

Asking someone to give feedback also solidifies their impression once they share it out loud. You should ask for feedback from people whose insights you value and whose advice you're more than willing to act on.

And because feedback is a gift, you should put some thought into how you ask for it so that the input you get is helpful. Everyone is better at providing a reaction to a situation with context vs. offering feedback in a generic way. We coach people to ask for feedback in the same way that we coach people to receive it.

EXAMPLE

Assume I'm a peer who is working with you on a project, and we've attended a few stressful meetings together. You know that you're struggling to keep the group aligned, and you want to know what others have noticed or think of you in that setting.

GENERAL – If you say: "What do you think of the project meetings?" you've left the topic up for interpretation, and my response may be anything from, "They're really frequent…" to "they run too long…" to "they're a lot of people who don't agree." I won't immediately offer feedback on how you're running the meetings.

CONTEXT – If you say: "I'd really appreciate your feedback on our discussion in the project meeting. Do you think we got to the right outcome or do you have any thoughts on how I could manage the group differently?"

Now I'll answer directly about the scenario and it will make it easier for you to expand the impressions and ask if others share my experience.

Here's what we mean.

If I say, "Well, I thought the discussion was more heated than it needed to be. You seemed to jump on Ed and John, and I think it may have shut down participation from others."

You could say, "Thanks for telling me that. I didn't realize that was happening. Have you seen that behavior from me in other parts of the meeting? Do you think I'm causing some of the meeting stress?"

The feedback started specific and now it's easier to ask about it in a broader context. Your colleague will either confirm that it's a behavior they've seen before, or express that it's just something related to the topic at hand. Always say "thank you" and, after you've worked on the behavior, circle back and ask your colleague if it's better.

This diffuses lingering impressions and sends the signal that you appreciated the feedback and have taken the input to heart.

Reacting to Feedback

Whether you ask for feedback or receive it as part of an assessment from your manager, everybody tries to answer it.

Feedback	Response
"You come across as disinterested in meetings."	*"Because I have no idea why I'm there."*
"You didn't seem to take much initiative with the last project."	*"Because I didn't get the logistics support I needed."*
"You don't seem very confident in customer meetings."	*"Because I'm not used to virtual presentations."*

How you respond to feedback is a clear sign of how receptive you are to an honest perspective. If you receive feedback as a challenge or a problem to answer, you'll shut down the honest perspective and you'll miss the most insightful part of feedback, which is what the person delivering the feedback feels is behind the impression.

In the examples above, whether or not you are disinterested in meetings, you're coming across that way. Whether or not you felt that you didn't have the logistics support to take the initiative on a project...there's an impression that you could have. And whether you're used to virtual sales meetings or not...you're coming across as timid and unsure.
Feedback is not meant as an accusation or a laundry list of complaints. It's an opportunity for you to understand the impressions your brand has created. Those impressions

exist, and whether or not you agree with them, the more you know about them, the more successful you will be in managing them.

When you signal that you receive feedback well, you can often get input on how to move beyond it.

EXAMPLE

Manager: You didn't seem to take much initiative with the last project.

You: Oh, that wasn't my intention. I'm sorry you had that impression. Can you tell me more about what you experienced?

Manager: Well, this was the first client project I really wanted you to spearhead, and it felt like you leaned on me every time you had a problem. It felt like you were hesitant about most of the logistics.

You: Thank you for sharing that with me. I can see how that may have come across. The truth is I am still a little unsure about our process around logistics. I'm really sorry I didn't meet your expectations on this last project. What's the best way for me to gain confidence with the logistics process? I thought about asking someone from logistics to join the project meetings, but I worried it was too late in our process to add them.

Manager: That's actually a good idea. I'll have you partner with Michael on this next project. Just make sure you're learning best practices from him and the rest of the team, so you'll be better equipped to lead another project.

When we approach feedback with the goal of understanding and learning, it creates a conversation that encourages the person giving feedback to share more rather than being cautious with their input. In this example, the conversation quickly gave you an opportunity to address your own concerns regarding your performance without being confrontational. You also managed to get what you asked for: the additional support from Michael.

Finally, this conversation with your manager gives you an opportunity to go back after the next project to see if you hit the mark and if your manager's impression of you has changed. Managers may not always remember all the feedback they've given to different employees, but they do remember the employees who take feedback, work to make changes, and circle back on feedback to see if they're improving. And when we challenge feedback instead of trying to understand it, they remember that, too.

In fact, challenging feedback makes it very easy for a manager to not give you feedback unless they have to. And when that happens, it limits your development very, very quickly.

Managing Feedback

Don't leave feedback unresolved with a manager or a colleague. Even though they don't like giving it, they remember it, and they will remember how you responded and what you did about it. No one's perfect; we're all growing and learning along the way. But we remember how people respond to feedback and our willingness to be honest is based on the receiver's receptiveness.

There is rarely a follow-up step for great feedback, but there is always a next step with poor feedback.

We coach people to defuse poor impressions, which can prevent a poor impression from becoming a lasting impression. When things don't go well, own it and try to defuse it.

So back to Hugh and the story at the start of the chapter. What could Hugh have done differently? If he considered feedback as a best practice, it would have been smart for him to ask for feedback and impressions before he transitioned to the second job. He could have asked his immediate manager for feedback like this: "John, I know that I came in at a chaotic time for the division and my role. How has that impacted initial impressions of my brand and my contribution to date?"

Or "John, it's been an unsettled start to my career here, and I know that most of that is attributed to the shift in structure and functions across the organization. But I also know that I haven't contributed as much as I would have liked. How do you feel that has impacted my start and the company's initial impressions of me?"

Words like "impressions" and "brand" tend to focus feedback on sound-bites that others have shared. Remember the description from Chapter 6! Your brand is how people think about you and talk about you. The comments above that refer to your brand are likely to draw out things that people have said about you.
So, we've created the need for feedback. Let's connect it to the rest of your brand. Chapter 3 gave you a visual way of thinking about impressions. The road map is a great way to

ask for feedback on your brand. In our brand workshops, we pair participants with colleagues who know them well, and we see what we described under Asking for Feedback. The triangle visual gives them something to react to rather than asking them to broadly share impressions. This is a good start to understanding how you're seen across your organization.

8

Brand Expectations Across a Career

In Chapter 5, we introduced our thinking on the phases of a career and how you should think about your skill set to keep your career moving forward. Now let's add into the mix others' expectations of your brand and what changes over the course of your career.

Early Career

This is the phase of your career where you should be most focused on yourself. Early-career employees gain visibility quickly, but you won't have the credibility that comes with experience. The expectations are for you to be open, interested, and earnest in wanting to learn and understand others.

At this stage, you don't have a proven track record, so people form impressions of you almost solely on how they experience you. In fact, when we hear clients give feedback on early-career employees, they talk about 1) their personal style and 2) how they observe them in a group setting.

We often hear early-career brands described in terms of likeability, capability, and adaptability. There's a lot of forgiveness for mistakes, missteps, and misquotes early in your career, and that's because people are more prone to notice how well you receive feedback and how well you take responsibility for any stumbles.

We hear a difference in someone who is "independent" vs. a "go-to" resource. We take note of who's described as "competitive" vs. "a team player." And we can distinguish between someone who a manager labels "reserved" vs. "collaborative." Can you? The second word in each comparison hints at someone who is working well with others. Managers notice this early on and they view it as an indication of leadership potential.

Coaching for early-career employees tends to focus on helping employees speak up more or helping them balance their directness by listening to others. Misconceptions form around self-focus, cockiness, and quietness. We use the foundational skills of presence to raise awareness of habits and help early-career employees build confidence.

Mid-Career

Your mid-career is the proving ground to becoming a leader, and it's where your focus needs to shift from you to everybody else. Your brand becomes harder to manage because peoples' experiences are different. In our coaching engagements, we gather brand impressions through a verbal assessment with a small group of people. Then we share the results back in a summary. And mid-career managers are always surprised when the insights we share are different than what they expected. This is often a reflection of someone who didn't pay close enough attention to how impressions were formed early on in their career.

When we hear feedback on managers in their mid-career phase, clients share insights on how others talk about them and respond to direction. This is where influence becomes the measurement of an effective communicator, and employees begin to clearly see the difference between someone who carries influence and someone who does not.

Brand impressions for mid-career managers are described in terms of leadership, influence, and clarity. We hear comparisons of "tactical thinking" vs. "strategic thinking," "a cheerleader" vs. "a coach," "in-the-weeds" vs. "a high-level communicator," and "someone who delegates well" vs. "a micromanager."

We hear a difference in these descriptors as well. The comparison illustrates the difference between someone who can motivate others to do things well vs. someone who gives orders but still owns the final product. Senior leaders who manage future leaders know that if you don't learn to delegate and trust others early, you'll struggle with an overloaded plate your entire career. Trusting others is a key factor in a manager's career and a shift from being a doer to a delegator and coach.

Coaching mid-career employees focuses on helping them learn to inspire others and manage different styles and personalities. An effective manager needs to know how to give honest feedback that helps someone move ahead vs. move away. Communication skills shift from foundational skills to integrated tools, and clarity of message becomes a true differentiator. A manager who can communicate effectively up, down, and across an organization is well-positioned to be a utility player who can move into multiple roles.

Peak Career

Expectations shift overnight on a senior leader. The expectations are greater as audiences get bigger, and even more so when you represent a full division or organization. Listeners don't just want to know what you're thinking, they want to know how you got there. It's no longer enough to say what you need from others; they need to know why it matters and where you're headed.

Brand expectations are aspirational. Employees want a leader who can galvanize thousands while making them feel a personal connection. They want a leader who is Hercules, Mother Teresa, and Braveheart, all in one. Leaders can be described as "aggressive," "demanding," "strategic," "knowledgeable," "charismatic," "empathetic," and "credible." And that's all just one leader! It's hard to be everything to everyone, and we tell leaders they don't have to be.

But they do need to understand the brand they've built and how it impacts different groups. While they don't need to change their entire brand, they can adjust their approach to make sure they can connect with any group. Communication becomes less of a toolkit, and more of an ingrained skill. At this point, communication choices should be instinctive and impactful.

Our coaching for peak career employees leans into storytelling and investing in what it takes to bring ideas to life and keep them alive over a period of time. It's the intrigue of the story, the memorability of the storyline, and the engagement with individuals that ultimately empowers a leader to connect with any audience.

Expectations expand as careers continue. But across all career phases, it's the experience of the brand that sets impressions. And the foundational skills of presence are the tools we use to help anyone drive consistency with impressions.

9

Presence: Three Key Attributes

If your brand is made up of impressions that have solidified over time, then in order to shift impressions you have to reset how people experience you. And most of those experiences and interactions are linked to you as a communicator. You may be communicating to influence a decision, communicating to disagree with a change, or simply listening to a discussion in a meeting. In all instances, you're considered a communicator.

That's because when two or more people are together, they form impressions as people speak up or listen in as part of communication. In fact, sometimes we notice as much about people who aren't talking as those who are speaking up. And to change those experiences, you need to know more about expectations.

We talk about impressions as 7:11. In seven seconds, people form an average of eleven impressions of a communicator. And because these impressions set quickly, they're strongly rooted in how listeners see and hear you.

Here are the facts:

- 55% of an impression is based on physical posture.
- 38% of an impression is based on the sound of your voice.
- And *only* 7% of an impression is based on the actual words you speak.

And when you think about it, this makes sense. It doesn't take long to notice that some people stand out and get noticed in a business setting. Whether it's a staff meeting, a client discussion, or even a social hour, we notice people who seem confident and comfortable. Those impressions are driven by an open and settled body and a full and measured tone to their voice. They seem confident, committed, and observant of others in the room.

When you encounter someone like this, you might say they have a strong "presence" about them.

And while we feel that our style and brands are unique and different than others in the room, everyone is pretty consistent in how they describe someone who carries influence in a meeting. And it suggests that we have consistent expectations of brands, even though the attributes may show up differently in individuals.

In our workshops, we ask participants to build a list of expectations and attributes they associate with presence. Their lists are always remarkably similar.

Here are the most common expectations:

Confident		Enthusiastic		Genuine		Connected	
Comfortable		Involved	Clear		Sincere	Knowledgeable	
Credible		Aware	Vested		Authentic		Honest
At Ease		Passionate		Thoughtful		Interesting	

As you look at this list, it may seem daunting to hit every expectation. How can someone be credible and interesting? Clear, but also thoughtful? All of the attributes are coachable and attainable. But delivering on these expectations feels different to different people. The attributes that are easy for you may take more intention from someone else. And that's the part that differs from one person to the next. It's taking the expectations and thinking about how they fit your brand and come across in your style. And ultimately, it means exploring intentional choices in how you use your body, your voice, and the listener to strengthen impressions.

There are three overarching themes that we use to represent listeners' expectations, and we call them the Three C's of Presence:

Confidence, Commitment, and Connection.

Confidence: A confident communicator is someone who seems comfortable, relaxed, and open. They seem at ease with people in any setting and that makes them appear clear, credible, and knowledgeable when they speak. They give the impression that they have the right to be there and can "own" any setting. We coach confidence as a physical concept, and we coach people to feel confident through posture, stance, and other concepts that allow someone to influence the physical space around them. This group of attributes drives 55% of an initial impression and the physical posture mentioned above.

Commitment: A committed communicator is someone who puts energy behind their thoughts. They are passionate about their ideas, which in turn makes them interesting to listen to. They're described as enthusiastic, involved, and vested in their thoughts. We coach commitment as effort and the best use of the voice, and we work with people on articulation, projection, and inflection to create warmth and interest behind their words. This group of attributes aligns to 38% of initial impressions and the sound of the voice mentioned above.

When you understand how to use your body and voice effectively, you become a competent and consistent communicator who can establish good impressions. Often when we form negative impressions, it's because we've misunderstood the choices someone makes about how we see or hear them.

But the ultimate goal of influence is to feel competent enough to shift the focus from your skills to your intentions. That's when you'll become compelling, because people notice that you can engage a room.

Connection: A connected communicator is someone who is focused on the listener's reaction and response. The focus shifts from how you are doing to how the listener is feeling. The connected communicator is actively involved with an individual or a group and seems to be focused on a listener's response. This effort and engagement leads to impressions of trust, sincerity, and authenticity. And while a confident and committed communicator can meet most listeners' expectations, someone who genuinely takes an interest in others is far more likely to be remembered. So, let's look at intentional choices that drive impressions across the three themes of style.

10

Attribute One: Confidence

Body language has a big impact on first impressions. Even if your body signals aren't intentional, it's hard for a listener to get beyond what they think your posture and your body are expressing. Posture means more than how you stand or look. It's how you use your body to convey a sense of openness and settled-ness to any listener.

When we ask people to define "presence," some of their favorite expressions are, "You know it when you see it" or, "There are some people who just own a room." Both expressions are a reaction to the physical-ness of someone.

Body language is both a mental and physical choice.

The mental portion is thinking through and accepting that being physically open means to be welcoming of everyone else's focus. And, to many people, the concept of being open translates to being vulnerable. That vulnerability is very real. Being the focal point of a room full of listeners can make you feel exposed. But listeners like people who are willing to be vulnerable with them. We like people who seem at ease with themselves and everyone else. The term "being comfortable in your skin" is a visual way of thinking about confidence.

How should you use your body to convey a sense of confidence? How does your body say, "I'm comfortable. I know what I'm talking about."?

- Ultimately, the lower body is settled and appears weighted and intentional.
- The upper body and arms are open, which invites focus.
- And the whole face is active and involved as someone speaks to us.

Here's how we get someone there.

Legs and Lower Body

People come in all shapes and sizes, and bad habits creep in to our posture to compensate for those differences. Someone who is tall will often try to diminish their size by sitting into their hips or dropping their shoulders. Someone who is heavy may cross their arms or narrow their stance. And someone who is petite often tries to fill the space with energy by moving around quickly.

People may fill space differently, but all of these habits get in the way of a settled and relaxed body, and the choices above can actually draw attention to the physical attribute you were trying to adjust. Instead, we'd coach you to think about a settled stance with even weight on both feet. This allows for a more balanced and weighted stance to prevent a lot of unintentional movement or swaying through the legs and hips.

The biggest detractor to confidence is moving one's body without purpose. Many nervous habits show up in movement – shaking a leg, twirling a foot, or fiddling with hair. When we see movement, we watch it. And no one wants to be remembered as the guy who shook his leg or the woman who fiddles with her hair! But these *are* noticeable habits. And you'll read more about them in Chapter 19, when we share insights on interviews from talent acquisition leaders.

Conversely, when someone seems settled and calm to us physically, we notice and listen to them differently.

Arms and Upper Body

The most important part of your upper body is your core or middle section. Most people mistakenly think it's the arms, because they worry about what their arms and hands are conveying. But arms and hands are attached to the core of the body and actually mimic what someone is doing with their core. The more open and involved the torso/core of the body is, the more natural the movement of the arms and hands becomes. We focus on helping you understand how to involve the core because we know the arms will follow suit. We call it "core engagement," and here's what it means.

When you communicate one-on-one with someone, you actually bring the core of your body toward them. Think about how you shake hands with someone. You move the core of your body closer to them, not just your hand. And that's true of any communication situation where you want to be seen as involved and vested in the conversation.

The core of the body plays a big part in conveying involvement and interest or conveying being closed and aloof. Consider someone you've seen who seemed interested in their topic and vested in getting their point across. Chances are, whether they were standing or seated, you noticed a forwardness about them.

Core involvement makes managing the hands a lot easier. The number one question we get about posture is, "What should I do with my hands?" Some people lock their hands to prevent movement, but locked hands block core engagement. The torso doesn't move or appears stiff when the arms are locked in tight, and it often leads to impressions of resistance or being closed or distant. You should use your arms naturally. It's our pace that drives rapid movement of our hands, not our physical choices. We'll talk through how to manage pace in our next chapter.

Head and Whole Face

If we have good habits with our physical choices, it shifts the focus away from movement and up to our faces. Think of it as shifting someone from watching you to listening to you. That's a really good outcome!

While the full body participates in communication, expressiveness and interest in you come from focus on your face and your expression. The balanced and settled body keeps the head level and conveys confidence; a tilted head or moving head can convey uncertainty or nervousness.

The three concepts of body working together deliver a settled stance, an open posture, and a warm and expressive face, which all add up to confidence.

These are intentional choices that lead to strong impressions. And while you may work on them or practice them in a private setting, here are some settings where you'll quickly notice an impact.

Group Meetings

Whether you're leading a meeting or participating in one, when you focus on posture, you'll immediately notice a difference in a room. The concepts above come to life as you watch who seems forward and involved in the conversation and who seems more pulled away and detached. And if you notice it, you can be sure everyone else in the meeting notices posture as well. To validate that, ask a few colleagues about their impressions of participants when the meeting wraps up. Notice how their impressions are linked to body language and how quickly they formed assumptions about participants based on what they observed.

Interviews

We've dedicated a few chapters to interviews, so we won't give away the insights here. But it's worth noting how important body language becomes in these high-visibility settings where every impression is a first one. It's hard to correct first impressions in this setting. Interviewers notice confidence, and they assess for it. It helps to have a strong sense of how to use the body to convey the impressions that you want the interviewer to take away.

Social Events

Some people say the most awkward brand moments are the big receptions and unstructured time to socialize and meet different people. It's hard to know how to stand in a large group and how to understand the impact of your body language across a room. All the notes on physical choices apply in this setting. In fact, we sometimes notice more about someone by looking at them across a room than across a table.

An open body that signals confidence is like a magnet for people. If your posture says that you're comfortable in a setting, people will approach you because they'd like to be comfortable themselves. Test it yourself the next time you're in a large group. Notice the difference in how people hold their bodies. Then, notice who seems to be drawing a small circle of attention. Their posture will be settled, open, and confident.

Presentations

The highest visibility situation is the stand-up presentation. You're the recognized focal point in this setting, and all eyes are on you. Most people feel a difference between seated and standing posture. You need to feel confident with both of them. Standing presentations require a good understanding of settled and grounded weight, so that movement stays intentional on your feet and can be just as involved as the seated and forward posture of a meeting.

Being confident is a physical feeling. People who use their bodies well can convey an impression of being knowledgeable, credible, and open in any setting.

11

Attribute Two: Commitment

If the body sets the immediate impression, the voice becomes an essential tool to keep a group's attention. When we hear commitment or tentativeness in someone's voice, we make assumptions about their confidence or uncertainty. When we hear a measured or rapid pace, we make assumptions about their purpose or lack of focus. Tone of voice conveys a lot of meaning behind words and can often make the difference between who is heard in a room and who is spoken over.

Overall, you want your voice to convey a sense of commitment, interest, and conviction. You want to be taken seriously with what you say and you want to be heard within a group. As listeners, we rarely distinguish between what's said and how it's heard. The quality of your voice has a lot to do with your ability to influence a listener.

Your voice adds impact in three different ways:

- Articulation, which sets the speech rate at a measured and intentional pace
- Projection, which delivers a full voice in a focused direction

- Tone, which signals to a listener how you want your thought to be received

Here's how we raise awareness of the voice and strengthen the skills of the voice.

Articulation

Energy is an interesting attribute to consider. Early in a career, having energy can be interpreted as being enthusiastic and willing to jump in. At mid-career, having energy can be perceived as being wound up and not focused enough to make a definitive point, being someone who just moves too fast. And at peak career, having energy is rarely a great attribute. When someone describes a leader as "high-energy," they often mean that they're a whirling dervish or someone who stays a little out of control.

In communication, energy used well best aligns to effort. Energy that seems out of control often aligns to pace.

Articulation drives effort behind the voice. It involves the use of the whole mouth, shaping the words for clarity and energy. You can observe articulation if you stand in front of a mirror and try this simple exercise:

- Watch yourself as you say the sentence, "I need the report at two o'clock." What you'll see this first time is your normal energy level.
- Now mix it up a bit. Repeat the sentence in a very flat or monotone way with no effort or inflection behind the words.
- Repeat the sentence a third time with full effort behind the words.

74

If you repeat the low effort and high effort deliveries a few times, you'll notice that the monotone sentence shows no expression or interest on the face, whereas the high effort sentence shows expression through your whole face.

Articulation drives expression, and, as listeners, we like communicators who are expressive when they speak. Expressive communicators are more interesting and are easier to listen to. Even when our hearing isn't impaired, everyone reads lips a bit when we are able to look at a communicator. And the more effort we see, the more commitment we believe.

Articulation also reduces filler words ("um"s, "uh"s, "like"s) and slows a rapid rate of speech by encouraging more effort.

Projection

Projection adds focus and intent behind the voice. Projection gets misunderstood as a voice skill because it's often associated with volume. While volume is a component of projection, you can be loud without having good projection.

When someone projects well, you'll think of them as focused, interested, and clear. It's the difference between talking *to* someone and talking *at* them. And if you watch a good communicator closely, you'll notice that when you feel as if someone is talking directly to you, they are actually sending their voice your way.

That's projection, and it supports the concept of forward intent called out in the last chapter (Chapter 10). In fact, projection actually leads the effort. When the voice is sent toward someone, it makes it very easy to bring the core of the body forward as well.

Projection starts with voice placement. Some people keep their voice in the back of the throat, which can result in a guttural or thin and raspy sound. It may be caused by tightness in the chest or just the habit of keeping the voice back. In most cases, the voice can be released and focused forward for a fuller tone.

Projection begins by getting the voice toward the front of the mouth. You can feel this by humming. When you hum, your mouth is closed, and you should feel a slight vibration on your lips.

Try this simple exercise to ensure that the voice is in the front of the face. Hum for about two seconds and then say a number as you open your mouth. "Mmmmm…one."

We describe this position of the voice as "out." You can feel the voice in the front of the face, and you can feel the voice expressed out in front of you as you said the number. This cleans up the guttural or raspy sounds made by voices that are held back.

Most people speak with the voice in the out position. They can easily feel the voice vibrate in the front of the face, and they assume that projection just means talking louder from there. But projection is a step beyond the space right in front of you. Projection is the intent to get the voice forward to the listener. Everything about good communication focuses forward, toward the listener, rather than holding back or keeping the effort of the voice around the communicator.

Here's a way you can experiment with projection:

- Find a room in your house or an empty conference room in your office.
- Using the full length of the room, line up chairs in three positions. The first chair should be close to you, the second chair should be half the distance of the room from you, and the third chair should be as far away from you as the length of the room allows.
- Stand in one spot and think about placing your voice in each chair. You can use numbers to get a feel for the exercise. Place "one" in the first chair, "two" in the second, and "three" in the third. Begin again by placing "four" in the first chair and so forth.

If you continue the exercise as you count to twenty, you will notice that it takes more effort to get your voice to the third chair. If you incorporate the physical concepts discussed in the previous chapter (Chapter 10), you should be able to feel the effort to project pulling the upper body forward. Projection drives core involvement.

When we project or place the voice with a listener, we align the core of our body with them as well. The voice and body are forward toward the listener, and this is what creates the listener's feeling that someone is talking to them.

Both of these technical skills help you set impressions of commitment, interest, and conviction. Articulation drives effort behind words, showing the speaker's investment in thoughts. Projection gets the words forward to listeners, indicating the speaker's interest in the listener.

Tone

Emotion is another interesting attribute to consider. We often describe people as "honest," "sincere," or "genuine," and these attributes can come across in the tone of someone's voice. We notice when someone seems to care about how we react to their words. We hear emotion or feeling in tone of voice, and it impacts how we hear something and how we react to the person who said it.

But when someone is described as "emotional," the impression has a very different meaning – and it often means that someone allowed how they felt to overcome what they wanted to say.

Tone of voice conveys the whole range of emotions, and it's helpful to understand how your tone is heard. You often can't remove emotion from your thoughts, and we don't think you should. But it's important to think about what you want the listener to do with emotion. When the thought and emotion are aligned, it comes through in the tone of voice. When the emotion is out of control and misaligned to the thought, it can be misread in the tone of the voice.

Here's an example:

Assume that you're working with a colleague on a project. You have both just been told that you need to accelerate the deadline for completion. You've been carrying some of your colleague's load because she had a lot of challenges pulling information from other teams. So, when your manager tells both of you to speed up the work, you say:

"Nancy can't get it done. She's had a tough time with all the dynamics of the project already."

As you say the statement out loud, assume that you are very frustrated with Nancy. You can probably hear a push in the tone of your voice and a little sarcasm. You can imagine the eye roll as well. All of that would send strong impressions to Nancy and the manager.

Now repeat the statement out loud and assume that you have great empathy for the challenges Nancy's been dealing with. You want Nancy and the manager to hear concern.

In the first example, Nancy would say you threw her under the bus. In the second one, she feels that you stood up for her. That's the impact of voice tone, and an important element of how impressions are set.

Developing voice skills can feel technical, and you may wonder how these elements impact your brand. Here are some settings where you'll quickly notice an impact.

Video Calls

The voice carries a lot of impact in a virtual setting. More on this in Chapter 13. Remember that any time the listener's experience of you isolates the voice from the body (conference calls, video conferences without video turned on, etc.), then impressions are set entirely by the sound of your voice. When we can't see someone, we base all of our impressions on the sound of their voice. People who have good projection and a measured pace to their voices always stand out on conference calls.

1:1 Conversations

Even with work colleagues, your voice becomes an imprint of your brand. Colleagues recognize your voice over the phone or down the hall. If someone were to describe you by the sound of your voice, do you know what they would say? Test it out with a good friend or close colleague. The words they use to describe your voice will be very similar to words they would use to describe your brand.

Difficult Conversations

Your tone of voice can betray you in more difficult conversations or when discussing more difficult topics. You may show emotion that you didn't realize you had about a topic, or you may become emotional when pressed on a topic. Most of these conversations work best if you've thought about what you want to say and then said it out loud to hear how the emotion comes through behind it. As you map out your thoughts, try to make note of the feelings behind your thoughts. This helps ensure that you present the two together in a manner that you're comfortable with.

High-Visibility Events

Most people realize the impact of their voice at the most revealing moments. It can be nerves before an important presentation or a catch in the throat standing on a big stage. Your voice can give you away quickly. Groups don't always see a physical response to nerves, but they can always hear a catch in the voice. And unfortunately, these high-visibility moments carry high stakes in terms of brand impressions.

Articulation and projection solve for most nervous responses, but you have to invest the time to learn how to use those skills consistently.

Your voice is a tool of influence. People who use their voices well convey an impression of conviction and effort. They can generate interest in topics and pull focus their way. We want to hear what they have to say, and we connect how we hear them to how we think about their brands.

12

Attribute Three: Connection

We touched on the topic of emotion in the last chapter as part of the discussion of voice tone, and in doing so we introduced the idea of thinking about how you impact others. The third element of presence, connection, is all about everyone else, and it calls out the ability to engage others.

In our workshops, people draft their brand maps as outlined in Chapter 6. The bottom left of the triangle, what you wish people would say, always has aspirational attributes. People want to be described and viewed as caring, thoughtful, sincere, likeable, and warm.

But unlike the body and voice elements of presence, connection isn't something you can practice or develop all alone, because it's all about everyone else. I can have thoughts about your brand related to how I've seen you or heard you without ever interacting with you. But in order to describe you as someone who is engaging, I would have to experience a connection with you myself.

When we wrote our first book on <u>Executive Presence</u>
a decade ago, we measured impressions and created a
hierarchy of the attributes people associated with leaders'
brands. The participants included early, mid, and peak-
career employees. The impressions that employees had from
seeing and hearing a leader filled the bottom to middle
section of the hierarchy. In some cases, these impressions
were based on what others had told them. But the top of
the hierarchy, the brand attributes that participants deemed
most important were linked to connection, attributes like
"authentic," "believable," "sincere," "intuitive," "empathetic,"
and "honest." This taught us two interesting things: first,
that employees valued those attributes the most, which put
them at the top of the hierarchy, and second, that employees
wouldn't credit a leader with those brand attributes unless
they had personally experienced them.

And that's why connection is the brand element that
leaders work on the most.

You can connect with words and thoughts. Leaders can
engage a room of a thousand with a keynote message and
vision. You can connect with a colleague over a shared lunch
or a cup of coffee.

The only thing you can't do to connect is fake it. As
listeners, we know what true connection is, and we know
what the experience of connection with someone else feels
like.

It's probably why it's the group of brand attributes that we
grade the toughest.

- "He acts like he cares...but he doesn't because he just reduced our team by four people."
- "She talks a good game when everyone is watching...but she never acts on the promises she makes."
- "She just doesn't listen...she always thinks she has the best ideas."

A lack of connection or the ability to authentically engage with people can be the hardest attribute to develop and the hardest misconception to change. It's a balance of listening, seeing, and reading responses. And while there are many ways to help someone establish a connection, our coaching begins with helping people think through what genuine connection really is.

Connection is one of those skills that most of us are instinctively good at in some situations. That makes it hard to replicate in every situation if you haven't taken the time to think through why it works when it works.

Here's a simple exercise to illustrate it.

Sitting across from a friend or colleague, share your weekend experiences. Notice how your friend or colleague responds to your recounting of the weekend. Chances are they're nodding at you, laughing with you, or exclaiming over a funny moment. If you let yourself really reflect on their responses, you'll notice that you were working for those responses, and your friend's laughter or interest encouraged you to keep going. In fact, you may have embellished an event or added more to the story because your friend seemed to be enjoying it. That's connection: the effort to draw a response from the friend, and the friend's reaction to you. It's a two-way relationship that includes verbal and non-verbal responses. You feel a response from your friend, and your friend feels that you're trying to draw that response.

Connection is very straightforward when you experience it one-to-one. But as groups get larger, communicators grow increasingly skeptical of the concept. In fact, they think that connecting with an audience requires a different approach than connection to a single person. They try to connect with a full group rather than talking to individuals in the group. So, they scan a room, glance in a general direction, or look over peoples' heads to the back of the room. But all these techniques defeat the point of connection: to read the interest and reaction of each listener. That's not something that can be done with a glance, and it certainly can't be done if you're looking at the clock on the back wall to avoid making eye contact.

Eye contact is a part of connection, but connection is more than looking at people. It includes an awareness of and interpretation of non-verbal cues and responses from listeners. Connection continues to happen at a one-to-one ratio, even in groups. We coach communicators to rethink how they connect with a group of fifty people. It is never one-to-fifty, or a communicator connecting with fifty people at the same time. It is always one-to-one, fifty times, which means a communicator talking to individuals in the group and connecting one at a time with fifty of them.

You've probably experienced this firsthand. A good communicator can make it seem as if they are talking directly to you in a room of a thousand people. And the reason is that the concept and effort of connection are still there. While a communicator may not literally be able to connect with one thousand people, they can make one thousand people feel connection, and it's because they continue to talk to individuals and work for responses, just like you did sitting across from a friend. As the communicator does this, it drives expression on the communicator's face that illustrates a conversational and authentic level of engagement. Listeners recognize that and respond to it.

We've talked a lot about vulnerability and confidence in personal styles, and connection is the group of attributes that challenges individuals the most. It means that you have to feel confident enough in your habits to shift your focus to someone else. It means speaking up in meetings or leading presentations with less focus on how you're doing and more focus on how others are feeling and reacting.

That shift in focus is difficult for communicators to make, but among the three attributes, connection is the one that is the most differentiating.

Here are some settings where you'll notice the impact of connection.

Discussions with your manager: Have you had a manager who didn't listen well? You would have noticed because in one-on-one conversations, your manager seemed distracted by their computer screen or was multi-tasking through most conversations. You felt that you were talking *at* them and not getting responses *from* them. Or your manager might tend to look at you but rush you with rapid nodding of the head that signals you to move along – and you do, finding yourself rushing through an update.

Are you this manager? As the employee or the manager, these examples illustrate how people feel when they don't get our full attention. The employee doesn't feel heard or recognized for what he's accomplished. A critical skill for every manager is learning to be present in a meeting so that people feel heard. It takes focus, patience, and active listening.

Project updates: Content can seem in conflict with connection when data gets heavy or you feel pressure to get information accurate. In presentations and discussions, communicators will often stay in their heads, working hard to get the facts right. When this happens, their faces become void of expression and most listeners focus more on the lack of connection they're picking up on than the details of what's being said.

This means that the speaker gets little credit for accurate information and can come across as being disconnected or being a talking head, especially when they don't engage others in a discussion. Communication is always about delivering information well. In fact, with a little practice, you will discover that talking to someone always makes presenting content easier.

A more formal setting, like a presentation to a large group, follows similar habits to those involved in the project update. Sometimes, it isn't the content that worries us as much as the large audience itself. Nerves kick in, and we become a little careful or closed as communicators vs. open and involved.

This creates impressions of uncertainty and tentativeness. The skill of connection can calm your nerves because it helps you shift the focus to others and balances communication as a two-way dialogue vs. the feeling that you're alone in the limelight. While listeners in a large group won't verbally respond to what you're expressing, they will react to you if you talk to them. Again, this takes practice, but connection is the element of presence that helps someone feel comfortable in the most high-profile of settings.

We've covered all three of the attributes of presence and how they can strengthen brand impressions. We're often asked how they show up in business settings, and here's what we've observed for many years.

Confidence is the boldest group of attributes. Because of that, confidence is table stakes in companies. Leaders must have confidence to lead people; young employees have to have confidence to gain visibility. Companies hold managers back when they don't have confidence, and they promote managers who do have it. It is an essential skill and expectation of leadership.

Commitment is the most varied group of attributes. People don't always understand how to use their voices, and they may stop short of trying to improve them. In many companies, there are managers who are confident but not very interesting. Employees notice this. They are less interested in seeing a low-energy manager take the stage or lead the meeting. In fact, this can be the point at which one manager gains more visibility than another, because companies like to put the more interesting communicators in the spotlight. Being able to create interest and motivate employees accelerates opportunities for leadership.

Connection is the most compelling group of attributes. When listeners talk less about their impressions of a leader and more about their connection to a leader, it's a clear signal that they've engaged with the leader and the storyline. While connection can feel like an elusive skill to develop, it brings in the attributes of presence that listeners admire most in leaders. When authenticity and sincerity show up in a leader's style, companies recognize that the leader can influence employees.

It takes all three attributes to drive impact. It takes confidence to earn the right to speak, commitment to build interest, and connection to engage someone else in a message or an idea. And when you understand how to deliver on all of these attributes, you're well on your way to build a compelling brand.

13

The Virtual Communicator

During the time we spent researching and writing this book, the world was turned upside down by the COVID-19 pandemic. Seemingly overnight, entire workforces shifted to a virtual format and everyone from early-career employees to peak-career leaders were left in an uneasy, unprecedented quagmire as the world shut down and worry spread. The future of their jobs was left uncertain, and, for many, jobs went away. This was the most disruptive time we've felt collectively as a modern workforce.

The disruption also drove transformation, and one of the lasting impacts was a shift to more virtual communication. Most employees were already familiar with virtual formats, and many participated in and led communication in this setting. But what they soon realized – and may still be realizing – is that they relied on in-person settings to create impressions. The virtual format was leveraged more often for follow-ups or touchpoints. Virtual formats were used to reinforce impressions, rarely acting as the *only* way to set an impression.

And when virtual spaces do become the full impression, it's harder. It's harder to onboard as a leader or an employee with only virtual contact. It's harder to influence decisions, and it's much harder to establish connection and draw responses from viewers. We quickly saw that people assumed the skills they used with in-person meetings would easily transfer to the remote setting. The reality is that some concepts transfer okay, while others don't at all. And the foundational skills of presence are impacted just enough to cause even the most confident employee to struggle a bit.

So now that we've explored the Three C's of Presence, it's worth highlighting how the concepts transfer or change in a virtual format. There are some nuances and additional blind spots that come with virtual communication. And while the rules of the game might change for virtual impressions, the stakes do not. In fact, they're raised even higher.

Listeners still form eleven impressions of you in about seven seconds, and you still have to be intentional about choices that drive those impressions, but your listener or viewer has more freedom and ability to disengage from you than ever before. In a virtual setting, a listener has complete control over the conversation. They may take your vital end-of-the-quarter sales pitch with them on their morning walk, a leader may mute your call to help children with their homework, or a team member may mishear your instructions while they multitask over laundry or cooking a meal.

And even when you have your listeners' focus on camera, virtual communication can be exhausting. Calendars are filled with back-to-back-to-back-to-back meetings and screen fatigue sets in without breaks. Virtual listeners seem to be exhausted, distracted, and rushed. This is a recipe for disaster from a communicator's standpoint! And that's why it's crucial to understand the nuances of virtual presence and how you can have an impact, even with a distracted listener.

Confidence

When the world shifted from conference rooms to virtual huddles, some people were excited about the new format. It was easier to feel confident broadcasting from your kitchen table rather than the front of a conference room. The tighter focus of virtual platforms reduced the feeling of exposure to a single, one-of-many square. For presenters who lack confidence or despise large-group settings, this is the silver lining of virtual formats. You don't need to own your space in a conference room when you can deliver the quarterly sales update from the comfort of your living room.

But, well, actually you do. It's just that in virtual settings, owning the space expands beyond your physicality to the physical space all around you. When you work in an office, you probably don't give much thought to the blinds in a window, or a glare on a screen. But when you're working from home, something as simple as a shadow over your face or glare on your glasses can distract listeners. The shift to virtual formats didn't shift how people form impressions or set expectations of you as a communicator.

While a listener sees less of you, they still expect the same attributes that portrayed confidence in an in-person setting, even in a virtual environment.

Virtually, being a settled and grounded communicator is as much about the environment on the screen as it is about you. If you're using greenscreens, they need to be used in front of flat, undisturbed surfaces. Dark home offices need to be lit by a ring light or other adjustable lighting. And the limited space you're given on the screen needs to appear open and relaxed, rather than cramped or constricted.

In Chapter 10, we told you that confidence is the boldest of all the presence attributes and that nothing you say can override what the body says to listeners. In a virtual setting, the same is true about your environment. No matter how interesting or insightful your content, if your background or surroundings are distracting or if there is too much noise or chaos in your home, no one will be able to hear you above the distraction.

Posture is still the focus when conveying confidence. Conveying confidence is easier seated, as we called out in Chapter 10. Be aware that virtual formats can make the view of you a little more two-dimensional, so, when you sit up straight, you actually appear rigid or pulled away. Forward intent is important on video and makes the difference in a viewer feeling as if you're talking to them. If you use your hands a lot, adjust the camera angle so that your hands are a part of the view, instead of dropping in and out.

Commitment

A distracted listener is a big challenge in a virtual format. Before the pandemic, the average American logged more than seven hours of screen time a day. Now, our brains are on a double-sensory overload, logging nearly double that number from increased Zoom meetings, client calls, and manager check-ins. So you're starting from a disadvantage with a distracted and mentally depleted audience.

What does pull a listener out of the virtual doldrums is the sound and effort behind the voice that we discussed in Chapter 11. The impact of voice conviction is higher in a virtual setting than when supporting an in-person impression. In fact, the importance of body language and vocal effort have almost been reversed in impact. When people are in a room together, you use body language to draw people's attention and keep it throughout a discussion. Virtually, the body *captures* attention, but the voice does more to *keep* attention.

Here's an analogy we use to describe how people hear things virtually.

Think of skipping a rock across the top of a pond. This game is about how many light touches the rock can make before falling into the water. If you think of the skips as your voice pattern, someone who talks too quickly skips through thoughts and never really weights a single thought. The listeners may hear specific thoughts, but they don't really "sink" in. Someone with a more weighted and intentional cadence would weight each soundbite as they speak, and this helps the point settle in with a listener.

In a virtual setting, people are separating the visual of you and the sound of you more than you realize. Even after you've created a welcoming and relaxed space to present or to talk from, you will frequently encounter listeners with their videos off who are clearly multi-tasking. This is where the weighted-ness of a voice comes into play. A weighted voice with effort and intent behind it will prick up the ear of a distracted listener and pull someone's focus back to your content. Remember that both articulation and projection help a communicator convey the attributes of commitment. Articulation drives the effort behind words, and projection gets the words forward to listeners.

Connection

Connection is still defined as a one-to-one engagement. In a virtual setting, there's only one listener – the camera – so it's most similar to a one-to-one conversation and, theoretically, it should become much easier to engage listeners. But we've found that translating the one-to-one connection to a virtual setting creates two challenges. First, it assumes that you understand the authenticity of one-to-one connection. This goes back to the exercise with a colleague or friend in Chapter 12. The challenge is that good connection habits have taught communicators to work a room, moving from one person to the next to make sure that every person in the room feels acknowledged and invited into the conversation. Translate that to the virtual setting, and you see a communicator talking to anywhere from six to twenty *Brady Bunch* squares. The communicator focuses from square to square to connect with each individual they see, unaware that the camera shot looks like a bobbing turkey as they move from person to person. So, connection doesn't translate as working a room in this way. It has to be one-to-one through the camera.

You have to think about drawing responses by talking to the listener through the camera lens. It feels narrower and colder, and it is. But if you understand the desire to draw response, you can still engage listeners with the expression on your face and the forward focus of your body and voice that illustrates an interest in talking to them.

The second challenge is the separation of the easy back-and-forth between a communicator and a listener. When you did the exercise in Chapter 12, it was easy to see the response you got from a listener, and you could feel the impact their interest or reaction to you had on your own effort and involvement in sharing the weekend experience. In a virtual setting, the back-and-forth of connection is clunky. It's still there, it's just harder to put the two components together. The viewers' experience of you is coming through a camera lens; their reaction to you shows up in the virtual square. So, you deliver the intent of connection through the camera, and you receive the listeners' response to you in the square.

You can do a lot to align the listener's view and your view by moving a camera to sit just above the virtual view of the listeners. But it isn't the same. It works best to be intentional about balancing your focus between the camera lens when you talk and the virtual squares when you listen. In fact, it can help to talk about what you're doing so the viewer understands the shift in your focus.

The virtual setting has forced a very close-up view of all of us, and we tend to zero in on someone's eyes. That's part of the fatigue. It takes more focus to look intently in someone's eyes vs. seeing all of someone. You can soften the view by backing up the camera a bit and drawing the focus to your full face and shoulders vs. the tight view of a face that fills the screen.

You can evaluate your own virtual connection and uncover bad habits by using any of the platforms you use regularly to make a recording.

Here's a simple exercise:

Pick a topic that requires a series of steps, like cooking a favorite dish. Start the video and tell your imaginary listener how to make the dish. Focus on getting the steps and details *exactly* right. You want to make the measurements precise and make sure you don't skip a single step. You're going for 100% accuracy, where your listener can follow your step-by-step instructions.

When you play the video back, notice what happens when you focus on getting the details right. You may see your focus shift by looking up or away from the screen. We describe this as being in your head and not present in the moment. You may even notice that your voice drops back when you do this and can sound pulled away. Think about impressions. Are you less focused or less confident? Do you seem unsure of what you're saying? Do you seem less intentional? Because of the close view, bad habits show up sharply. This is caused by the focus on getting it right.

Now, make a second video. Shift your focus from getting it right to describing the experience of cooking, and sell that experience directly to the camera. Is this a recipe you make every year with your grandmother? Is it a family tradition with secret ingredients? Focus on creating interest and drawing a response to this great recipe. When you play back the video, you should notice a change in focus and facial expression. When you talk directly to the camera, it feels as if you're talking directly to the listener. And when you focus on creating interest, you can see your own interest. Those are the foundational skills of connection – you just get there a little differently through a virtual format.

When our shift to virtual workspaces originally started, most people were quick to say that they could easily adjust to the virtual format. But over time, most have admitted that they miss the natural connection that comes easily sitting across from someone. People miss the energy they draw collectively from groups. This highlights the value of in-person impressions and the ability to take in the whole person vs. such a narrow snapshot.

Virtual communication changes who has control over a conversation. And most of us are just not used to people connecting and disconnecting with us so easily. It makes communication feel disjointed. But you can gain more control by adjusting your style to the virtual format.

Virtual settings are a bit of a juggling act, and this reasserts the even greater importance of presence in a virtual setting. Virtual communication is its own unique medium, and it requires its own set of skills. They aren't totally different, but they aren't as easy as they may seem. And as you rethink your brand and your career, mastering the virtual setting will be an important skill to add to your toolkit.

14

Building a Brand (Early Career)

In the early phase of your career, your brand is only about one thing: you. How people experience you in between meetings, how you interact with them on Zoom or walking down a hallway, and how well you seem to listen and play well with others. And that's because, at this point in your career, your brand is the only thing you have to stand on. Your accomplishments in the workplace may not carry enough weight yet, and your college GPA and resume don't matter much to a manager who is trying to decide whether or not to give you more responsibility.

In fact, when managers look for an early-career employee to delegate to or promote, they're looking based on reputation as much as anything else. Would your colleagues say you were honest, hardworking, and dependable...or are you difficult, argumentative, and a know-it-all?

And while every person's career path is unique, we've worked with enough early-career individuals to know some common pitfalls that occur when people don't pay attention to their personal brand in the early years.

Here are a few stories that illustrate the impact of brand and coaching to help you get beyond a misstep.

Misinterpretation of Feedback

As we mentioned in Chapter 7, feedback is a gift and the best way to understand how you come across to others. Whenever possible, you should ask your manager for feedback and work together to identify and address any concerns. Sometimes feedback can be misinterpreted, and that can be just as harmful in the long run as receiving no feedback.

This can happen at any career stage, but we see it most often in early careers because employees don't have the experience or the coaching to understand the nuances behind difficult feedback. They may misinterpret their manager's gentle feedback as a sign that everything is fine, only to be confused and disappointed when they're told they haven't shown improvement during their next review. Or they may interpret hard feedback as a personal rejection and either lack the confidence to try new strategies or begin to seek a new role with a different team.

Here's Mia's story:

Mia recently transitioned to a new company after three years as a sales rep for a software firm. She had a successful track record in sales and came highly recommended by her manager. She was a great candidate during the interview process, and her new company was excited about the impact they thought she would bring to her new team.

About six months into her new role, she had her first review with her new manager. They made small talk for a while, and he asked her how she liked the role. She replied that she loved it and really thought that she was learning the business and making great strides.

Her manager nodded and gave her a half smile as he said, "Well, Mia. You sure are *passionate*."

The review wrapped up after another ten minutes and Mia left feeling great about her role and the success she was having. But two years later, she was still in the same role.

In every review her manager continued to tell her how "passionate" she was, and Mia assumed that meant he saw the energy she brought to her role. She heard it as a positive statement. It took her another year to realize that she had hit a real roadblock, and she still didn't understand why.

In working with Mia, it became clear to us that her manager used the word "passionate" to describe a style that was very aggressive. And because the feedback was vague and she wasn't making progress, she was offered some coaching time with us.

Here's what we learned. Prior to working for this company, Mia had worked in an industry where she learned to be aggressive because the sales cycle was tough and turnarounds were tight. So when she heard her new manager call her "passionate," she heard it as praise for results and her energy. In reality, the new company was a different culture, and her style was holding her back. Her colleagues didn't appreciate her "sharp elbows," and her manager was worried she was rubbing clients the wrong way.

He tried to give her that feedback without being confrontational, calling her "passionate" rather than "aggressive." Through coaching, we got to the root of the feedback and helped both Mia and her manager talk more honestly with each other. The original feedback might have been delivered with the best of intentions, but it was misinterpreted. And it took Mia more than a year to get back on track.

The same thing nearly happened to Nigel:

Nigel was part of a leadership program that brought a cohort of emerging managers together for development over the course of a year. We were a part of the multi-step curriculum.

Nigel was easily the most outgoing guy in the room, and probably the smartest. The only problem was, he acted like it. Over the course of the program, participants had several opportunities to give each other feedback. Nigel's colleagues consistently told him he came across as smart, direct, and articulate. What they never said was that he was genuine, authentic, or even likable. He didn't hear the difference.

In each session, Nigel was always the one who spoke first. He didn't seem to hear the undertones of his peers' feedback or notice the non-verbals exchanged by everyone else when he monopolized discussion. His brand was rubbing them the wrong way. And while his peers' feedback was somewhat muted during the in-person sessions, their feedback was quite clear in the anonymous survey at the program's halfway point. Most labeled Nigel a know-it-all, overly confident, and unpleasant to work with. Nearly everyone listed him as the person they'd least like to work with.

Feedback is hard. It just is, whether you're giving it or receiving it. And in order to avoid hurt feelings or messy discussions, managers and colleagues may soften remarks by being less direct or disguising negative feedback with praise. As a result, the feedback may not be heard, or the employee may underestimate its importance.

In Mia's case, misinterpretation of feedback stalled her career. Her manager was trying to gently deliver difficult feedback. It was likely that he didn't feel comfortable giving Mia hard feedback, and so she misinterpreted his attempts to "soften the blow."

In Nigel's case, his colleagues either didn't feel comfortable voicing their full concerns or didn't feel like Nigel would listen to them, so their frustration bottled up until it was time for the midway reviews. The review and the program gave Nigel a chance to think about his brand and reset impressions with his group. And while it wasn't easy, it provided a good environment for Nigel to work with his colleagues and shift impressions.

The majority of us bring a "grin and bear it" approach to feedback, whether we're giving it or receiving it. But you have to approach feedback as a conversation, rather than a confrontation. Managers don't like giving feedback, and the truth is that few are good at it. If they sense you're uneasy, they'll clam up quick. Don't challenge input; seek to understand it and expand it.

Ask for examples to understand where the impressions originated. If Mia had done this early on, she would have understood what the broad term "passionate" really meant.

In Nigel's case, his brand stood out quickly, it just didn't align with the traits he expected. He was quickly labeled as smart, but not a team player. He needed to learn how to read a room and understand how his comments were received. Observing more and talking less helped him a lot. It was hard for him to ask for more insights from his peer group, but he did it. And it changed both his relationship with the group and his understanding of his brand. Today, he's a much better communicator because of it.

Poor Impressions, Lasting Impressions

Everybody makes mistakes. We say the wrong thing, or we just show up in the wrong way. What matters most in these situations is the ability to recognize mistakes and take ownership for how to correct them. And it's remarkable how little we actually do that! Taking ownership for missteps has almost become more of a differentiator than an expectation. Yet when we allow a mistake to sit unresolved, it can grow into a poor and lasting impression.

Here's Renae's story:

Renae worked with her boss Patrick in account management. Patrick had a colleague, Cliff, who worked in an adjoining department. Patrick and Cliff were asked by their boss to look into solving an accounting problem for which they shared responsibility, and they had conflicting opinions. They didn't see eye-to-eye, so Patrick looped Renae in to help him refine their department's recommendation.

This account was an area of expertise for Renae, and she did not think that Cliff's strategies made sense. She said as much to Patrick...on an email chain where Cliff and their boss were also copied. Patrick jumped in to cover Renae's mistake and supported her concerns with Cliff's proposal.

Renae's note triggered an immediate response from their boss questioning Cliff's points, and, after a little back-and-forth, Patrick's strategy was adopted for the account. Renae felt great about her contribution and appreciated being looped in to a high-level strategy meeting. But Cliff did not forget that way she handled her input. He felt humiliated.

Fast-forward three years, and he still hadn't forgotten. When an opportunity came for Renae to join a new division as a director, she was blocked by the division's VP... Cliff. He had held on to that feeling of being humiliated, and he saw the promotion as an opportunity to get even.

Cliff's reaction might seem petty, and it is. But it's a real reaction and it happens all the time. From Cliff's perspective, his only interaction with Renae was via email when she embarrassed him in front of his boss. To Cliff, she was arrogant with her comments and quick to demean someone else's ideas. His impression of Renae was not a good one, and because there was no explanation or apology, Cliff held on to that impression of her brand until they crossed paths again.

<u>Something similar happened to Bobby:</u>

…Only in Bobby's case it happened at the company Christmas party. Everyone was having a good time and blowing off steam after a successful sales year. Bobby's company was still run by its founder, Paul, who was something of a personal legend around the office. Paul was your typical self-made man. He had founded the company twenty years ago and was still the acting CEO.
Neither Bobby nor anyone on his team had met Paul personally, but they had seen him from a distance when he'd visited their branch a few months earlier. He talked to all employees that day in a very relaxed and conversational way, so they felt like they knew him. After all, this was Paul's company, and the "Paul-stamp-of-approval" was a common reference point across the sales team.

Fast-forward to the party. Paul approached a group that included Bobby. Bobby clapped Paul on the back and said, "Hey Paul, it's great to see you! We did it, man!"

Paul frowned, but Bobby didn't notice. Paul nodded politely and spoke to the team for a few minutes before moving on. What Bobby didn't notice was that Paul was offended by the slap on the back and familiarity from someone he didn't know. And he didn't forget it.

Whenever someone brought up Bobby's name for promotion, Paul would say that he didn't think Bobby was very professional or that "he wasn't ready yet." This continued for four promotion reviews before Paul ever mentioned to anyone what specifically bothered him about Bobby. In fact, it took Bobby's manager asking Paul one on one what was wrong before Bobby ever found out about the misstep.

Over the course of your career, you may misstep. Poor actions may not be as clear as Renae and Bobby's, or as drastic. But at some point, your actions may rub someone the wrong way. And chances are, you'll see the response if you're paying attention. You'll notice if you've fallen out of step with someone. But the bigger miscue is doing nothing about these poor impressions.

Lack of awareness of a mistake is more damaging than the mistake itself. And it's easily solvable: always close the loop. A misstep is a simple hiccup when you acknowledge it and move beyond it, but when you leave it unacknowledged, it becomes an impression. And as these stories illustrate, once an impression sets in, it's much harder to move beyond than a simple misstep.

Getting Noticed

We mentioned in Chapter 8 that early-career employees gain visibility quickly. This comes from a diverse set of responsibilities, an active learning curve, and rotation programs designed to give employees a view of different functions of a business. It's a big opportunity that most employees want to know how to make the most of.

There's an art to signaling your interest in a conversation, even when you're not the focal point. It's the difference between someone who seems active and vested in a topic and someone who doesn't. It's about confidence and interest, and it's a skill that's rarely taught to young professionals. But it gets noticed.

<u>Here's Paige's story:</u>

Paige was invited to a senior-level meeting with her boss, Michael. Paige was the subject-matter expert (SME) on a particular marketing initiative, Alpha, that Michael's team was running, and Michael took her to the meeting in case his presentation went deep into details. When Paige walked into the meeting, she sat on the outer circle around the conference table with the other SMEs while Michael stood up to give the presentation. They had agreed that if questions delved into details, he would pull her into the conversation to answer the questions.

It never happened. Michael knew the topic well enough and the leaders' interest never veered into Paige's lane. The agenda moved ahead, and Paige was a little disappointed. It was her first executive-level meeting. She had been nervous about it, but then disappointed that her moment of visibility came and went without her saying a word. But she couldn't get up and leave the meeting, so she had to wait till the next break, about an hour later.

Paige started thinking about some of the coaching from our workshop. She decided to make the best of the hour and, instead of disconnecting from the discussion, looking at her phone, or responding to email, she took an interest in the meeting. She leaned in a bit and listened with interest to the discussion of the next topic. And when break came an hour later, she left without being noticed at all – or so she thought.

Before she got to the elevator, she heard someone behind her say, "Excuse me. Are you on Michael's team?" She looked up and realized it was the Chief Marketing Officer (CMO).

She said yes, she was on Michael's team, and he said: "I thought so. You were here to back up the discussion of Alpha campaign, right? I was really impressed with your work. I noticed you across the room and you seemed vested in the topic. I'd really like to know more about the campaign. I didn't want to take Michael's time to get the details, but would you have time to walk me through it next week?"

Oh yes, she did! Paige's initial meeting with the CMO was a high-visibility moment. It led to work on three additional projects for his team. Within six months he pulled Paige over to his team, two levels up above her previous position. In short, a visibility moment where Paige thought she was invisible turned out to be an opportunity to be intentional about impressions. The CMO saw interest, and she stood out.

True, Paige's work on the campaign was well-done, and that was what originally put her on the CMO's radar. But he might not have noticed her if she'd seemed checked out with her head down in her email. This story may sound like a movie, but it's a true story. People notice people who are more intentional about how they show up.

Getting Lost in the Crowd

In your early career, you join a team and settle in to learning new skills and contributing toward that team's goals. And in the process of settling in, you can miss the team dynamics happening all around you.

Most managers will, at some point, be asked to rank their teams. It may be in a formal review process or even just anecdotally in conversations about promotion candidates, but they'll be asked to think about the individuals on their team and their skill sets in terms of strength and competency – and sometimes even just likability! So, if your manager had eight people on their team, and they were asked to rank your team members one through eight, do you have some sense of where you would fall on that list?

We help people think about impact and visibility with the following questions.

> *Question #1: If your manager ranked her team in terms of value to her organization, would you be in the top third of the team?*
> *Question #2: Would you be in your manager's top three? And Question #3: Are you your manager's right-hand person?*

We walk through this exercise to make a point: your manager cannot champion everyone on their team. While they can *manage* everyone, they can't create the same level of visibility and opportunity for all eight of their direct reports. Usually, managers get focused on promotion and success of one, two, or possibly three people on their team. They focus on the ones who stand out, the ones whose brand is inviting and accepting of feedback, and the ones who seem diligent, earnest, and collaborative. You want to be in the top three.

If you don't think you are, the best way to advance is by asking for feedback. Start a conversation with your manager about impressions. The best way to reset your brand is to show your manager and your colleagues that you're trying to reset.

15

Building a Brand (Mid-Career)

In some ways, the priorities of your brand carry over from early career to mid-career. You need good awareness of your brand, frequent feedback, and the ability to correct missteps. The difference is that now your career comes with more risk and more reward, so your team plays a critical role in your success.

In your mid-career, you should have more opportunities for visibility to company leaders. Even in large organizations where there are layers of reporting, you should be valued enough that you're needed from time to time in executive-level conversations. The visibility of your brand is elevated across an organization. Talent discussions begin to look for the company's next emerging leaders, and your leaders will take note of impressions from those executive-level conversations. Some personalities emerge as front-runners, and companies develop a shortlist of high-potential (Hi-Po) managers they see as future leaders.

But not only do talent development leaders pick up on these strong brands... your colleagues do, too.

We support many Hi-Po programs with training seminars and coaching. Most of these programs are for seasoned managers and directors, with twenty-five to thirty people in a cohort. Few of them know each other when the leadership program begins. Most programs run nine to eighteen months, and by the time we work with a group, they've usually been together for one or two seminars.

As part of our engagement, we ask participants to complete an assessment on themselves as well as their colleagues in the program. We gauge impressions with questions like, "Whose brand really stands out to you?" and, "Who would you most want to work with?"

In each group, similar patterns emerge. Mid-career brands are *quite* noticeable, especially in a peer group of Hi-Po candidates. Consistently, groups name only three or four people. The responses are scattered across the whole group. It's not about who they sat beside in the first meeting or who they've partnered with in exercises, it's who the group has already recognized as an emerging leader in the group setting. And once they've identified the strong brands, they answer the rest of the survey questions with the same person.

Very quickly, whether in a group like this or across a company, compelling impressions begin to establish someone as a future leader. Their peers believe that they *will* be a leader, and they identify them as someone they would like to work with. As you can see, within just a few months of beginning a program, the group has already identified future leaders – and most of those impressions stay consistent throughout the program.

That's great if you happen to be one of those three or four managers with a compelling brand, but that fast track doesn't happen for most people. In fact, mid-career is where a lot of managers feel "stuck." That's because the expectations of you and your brand have changed. The shift from being an individual contributor to a manager brings unexpected challenges, and how you deal with them and adapt to changes can position you in one of two camps: a competent manager or a compelling leader.

There are some unforeseen pitfalls for mid-career employees. The stories that follow can help you consider situations that you need to work through or leverage to help your career continue to advance.

From Back to Front

In your early career, most of your contributions happen behind the scenes. Sales can be an exception to the rule, but even young sales professionals don't lead large customer conversations solo. In mid-career, many managers shift from behind the scenes to the forefront.

That's a huge shift in expectations. Your role is less about the work and more about influencing the work of others (and being held accountable for the work of others). You spend as much time communicating about work as managing the work itself. That's a new skill that many managers aren't prepared for.

Harry certainly wasn't.

Harry was a Manager of Data Science who was promoted to Director when his colleague Joe left the company.

As part of the new role, Harry took on responsibility for Joe's accounts, which represented several high-profile relationships for the company. Joe had managed these accounts for eight years, and Harry had partnered with him for the last year. Harry was familiar with clients' needs and had been supporting Joe's presentations with data and insights behind the scenes.

Yet when the transition occurred, Harry quickly sensed that he was missing the mark. His new clients interrupted him on calls and seemed to challenge a lot of what he said. Client issues were now taking three or four calls to resolve, where they had only taken Joe one or two. It wasn't long before Harry's boss took note. She started to have some of Harry's clients reach out to her directly instead of going through Harry. She was involved in many more client conversations than she had been with Joe. This wasn't sustainable for the company, and that's when we were brought in to work with Harry.

Here's what was happening: Joe and Harry were very different people. While Joe had been outgoing, high-energy, and gregarious, Harry was low-key, quiet, and analytical. He was every bit as nice a guy as Joe, and no one had anticipated a difficult transition with the accounts.

But how Harry showed up with clients was different. His voice was a bit shaky and lacked energy, which caused him to come across as nervous and less credible. In his previous role, he lived and breathed data analytics, and his role was to explain the details of a concept. His instinct was to go straight to the data of a situation, rather than explaining the story behind the numbers. It was where Harry was most

118

comfortable, and he didn't adjust his approach in the new role. This confused and frustrated his clients, who wanted a more holistic view of their accounts. Harry was still thinking like an analyst and, for him, this was a hard habit to break.

Moving from behind the scenes to front and center is a concept that many managers believe they understand. They expect the extra responsibilities and the longer hours, and they look forward to the opportunities of exposure and continued promotion. But managers can miss a communication expectation that shifts overnight. You don't communicate with just one boss anymore…you now have to communicate across an organization. And not in the detail that makes sense to *you*, but in broader concepts that connect ideas to a diverse group of leaders.

We see this challenge frequently in companies with fast-paced growth. Managers are moving up quickly because of their ability to understand a project or an initiative. They get promoted because they're good at what they do. But as visibility increases internally or externally, someone's ability to communicate clearly is suddenly put under the microscope.

In Harry's case, he had never had to align insights to business outcomes and impact, and he struggled with this. When we worked with him, we were able to introduce new skills to elevate his conversations with clients and strengthen his style to come across as more confident and credible vs. withdrawn and tentative.

At the mid-career level, the ability to shift focus and communication from a tactical view to an enterprise one is confusing to managers. Over the years, they've become subject-matter experts, and their value was known and measured against that expertise. But as leaders get more exposure to managers, they start to value someone who has a broader view and seems to be a strategic thinker.

In order to shift your brand from being a tactical manager to a more strategic one, you have to learn how to raise the altitude of communication and focus on what listeners need and value. Harry was still acting as an analyst in a director's role. He had to understand the shift and work quickly to reset his brand and move beyond the analyst mindset.

Impressions Haven't Progressed

By mid-career, talent reviews are no longer performed by a single leader. They're done by committee. Promotions are as well. And that's because, for the company, the stakes get higher. They want to make sure they've got the best person in the role, and they're beginning to evaluate managers as future leaders who can move up and across an organization.

In the early-career stories, we shared an example of understanding whether you're in the top three people a manager would champion. At mid-career, it takes more than one champion. Once reviews and promotions become committee decisions, your brand has to be known outside your leader's department. Your boss' peers need to know you and your work. If your VP were to put your name forward for a role today, how would the VP Finance and the Chief Revenue Officer react? Would they be comfortable with the decision…or skeptical? We see many careers stall in these sessions because people across the business just don't know a manager.

Building relationships across an organization can be a blind spot for mid-career managers. Sometimes, it happens easily with high-visibility meetings. In fact, that's why managers are often pulled in to these meetings. But it also helps to be intentional about building relationships. In our coaching work, we begin an engagement by asking mid-career managers about key influencers. We want to know if they know who has the ability to impact their career, and we want to know how strong the relationships seem to be. A key coaching goal may be to strengthen their brand impression with a few of those influencers.

When someone gets stuck, it's usually because they haven't paid attention to how their brand has evolved across a team or a company.

<u>And in Madison's case, it was personal.</u>

Madison had just been promoted. Overnight, she went from being a colleague to being the boss. And the trouble started immediately, because she happened to be really good friends with her team. Not just "work friends," but social friends with nearly everyone on the team. She was promoted to VP Customer Success on a Friday, and on Monday morning, she was the head honcho in charge of her closest friends.

The first thing she experienced was that her friends were jealous that she got the role. They had worked well together as colleagues, but as soon as the decision was announced, her "friends" challenged Madison on everything. And while most of it was just venting, Madison took it personally. She quickly adopted the wrong approach: she tried to lead like she was still one of the gang.

She tried to please everyone, talking to them as friends, which is what she'd always done as their colleague. By acting as a friend, Madison was able to move the group beyond hard feelings about who became the boss. But her "friends" quickly saw an opportunity to take advantage of her. Because she was leading like a friend, her team felt it was fine to show up late for work, to take an extra vacation day, and to interrupt work for personal calls. With the best of intentions, Madison had set up an environment where everybody thought she was a pushover. Her boss noticed, and so did other VPs within the company.

This is where our coaching relationship with Madison began: managing tough conversations. In one particular instance, she couldn't get beyond being taking advantage of by one of her good friends. The friend didn't take feedback seriously and continued to take advantage of Madison. We coached Madison for a tough conversation that presented two choices for her friend: move to a different department or work through a performance improvement plan. It was a tough learning experience for Madison, and it damaged her brand with her boss. It took a lot of effort and about nine months to reset her brand with the team and her boss.

Going from being a colleague to being a boss is a tough step that happens frequently throughout your career. We coach managers to recognize that people can't change their perspective on you overnight, but you can change the way you interact with them. The key is to be intentional about what will be different. This feels counterintuitive; most managers think they can keep everything the same.

But in order to establish yourself as a new leader within your organization, you need to do the opposite. You need to send intentional signals and reset relationships. As the manager, the burden of reset is on you because you're the role and individual who has changed. You can't expect everyone to see you differently overnight, but you can set an intention for a different relationship. It's an honest conversation that allows colleagues who may be friends to voice their concerns and work through the ground rules of a new relationship with you.

In Madison's case, she had to be clear about conversations that were appropriate for her friends to have with her, and ones that were not. You earn a team's respect over time, but to do so, you have to show up like a manager the day that your position shifts. And because Madison hadn't considered this, her brand struggled with impressions in the first several months of her new role.

The Supporting Role

Fast pace and frequent change create temporary gaps in companies. Many internal promotions are created because someone moves on, and talent teams would tell you that this creates great opportunities for mid-career managers to advance. We've shared stories about the value of being the right-hand person to a leader because it positions you for visibility. If early-career employees are working to establish credibility, mid-career managers are working to establish their value. And being in the supporting role to a leader is a great way to prove that value – unless you work with a leader who takes advantage of you.

<u>Consider Andrew's story:</u>

Andrew was a Senior Director in a large Silicon Valley firm. A position became available for a senior leadership position within the company, but the hiring committee wasn't quite sure if Andrew was ready for the role. They thought he was close, but not quite ready. So, they brought in a new leader from outside the company, Chris, and Chris became Andrew's new manager.

From the start, Chris was a weak leader. He knew nothing about the business, so he leaned heavily on Andrew day in and day out. Most new leaders need a close alliance with someone to learn the ropes for their first hundred days, but Chris relied on Andrew well beyond that timeframe. Andrew attended every meeting with him, he delegated most projects to Andrew's supervision, and he sought Andrew's direction on most strategy decisions. As this went on, Andrew felt taken advantage of. He felt he was bearing the responsibility of the senior leader role that the company thought he wasn't ready for, and that Chris was getting recognition for Andrew's work.

It's a tough scenario. Being in the supporting role and being the right-hand person to a leader is the best way to learn, and it's a fast way to create value. But there's a difference between creating value and allowing yourself to be taken advantage of.

So, what do you do? First, you talk to Chris about it. Through our coaching session with Andrew, we learned that Chris was a nice guy, though a weak leader. When Andrew talked to him about it, Chris acknowledged that he relied on Andrew too much and he made promises about shifting the workload. He just never did. The current pattern just worked too well for Chris.

By the time we talked to Andrew, he was frustrated. He was exploring opportunities outside the company and felt the only way to advance was to move to a different place. What a loss that would have been for the firm! We realized that Andrew needed to create awareness of the situation without telling on his boss. This is where the network of influencers comes into play. Andrew was well-connected to Chris' peers and often worked with them. So, we coached him to look for opportunities to let Chris' peers know that they were seeing his work on key projects. The goal was not to claim credit, just to align credit. We also coached him to be patient in waiting for the peer group to pick up on it.

One senior leader did. Andrew was working on a project that collaborated with another leader, and it became Andrew's opportunity. In their meetings, Andrew began to take ownership for elements of the report. Instead of saying, "we think," he said, "I thought." Instead of saying, "we looked at," he said, "I looked at." It was a gentle shift from the team tone of "we" to the more direct ownership of "I."

It was a risk of sounding self-centered vs. revealing personal ownership. But Andrew knew this leader, and the leader knew Andrew. And after a few meetings, the leader seemed to hear what Andrew was saying. In fact, he asked Andrew very directly: "Andrew, it sounds like you've built this strategy, instead of Chris. Is that true?" Once he piqued the leader's interest, the story unfolded from there. The leader asked questions, and Andrew responded to them. He never had to put forward Chris's shortcomings himself.

Andrew never knew what happened from there, but we suspect the peer used those insights to shine a light on Chris' gaps in other settings. A few months later, Chris was no longer with the company.

In most cases, the supporting role is the best place for a manager to be. It signals that a leader sees value in you, and you've established trust with the leader. And if you find yourself in the rare instance of feeling taken advantage of, think through a strategy that helps you illuminate the uneven balance of the workload. It takes patience and more than one trusted relationship.

16

Building a Brand (Peak Career)

In peak-career roles, the stakes continue to rise with higher expectations and greater risks. And this shows in the retention rate of CEOs. Historically, companies could have a career CEO for ten to twenty years, but the long-tenured role has quickly changed. For publicly traded companies, the average CEO tenure is under five years, and that means 17% of public companies are changing CEOs within a given year.

Often, the reason for turnover is self-inflicted. Missteps become blunders, and at a peak-career level, they are very visible and very public. In fact, you've probably seen several of these episodes play out in the news. They run the gamut from a leader saying the wrong thing at the wrong time to allegations of misconduct. It's hard for a senior leader to recover from a widely seen blunder, and many don't. The leading cause of dismissal for CEOs is ethical lapses (39%), outpacing even a company's financial struggles and CEO–Board struggles.

The reason why missteps are so costly is that a peak-career brand is synonymous with a company's brand, and few companies can afford to let the tarnished brand of a leader bring down the brand of a company. Companies are intentional about aligning brands. It's why young or struggling companies might bring in someone with a strong and established brand to add credibility to a company's brand, or a seasoned company may bring in an unknown leader to align a new and innovative direction for a brand.

Some missteps in a peak career are related to ego. Peak-career positions are powerful, and some leaders can get a little too focused on believing that a company's success was driven by their actions and achievements. When confidence crosses over into arrogance, it can be the beginning of the end for a senior leader. In fact, leadership at the top level requires just the opposite. Top leaders drive influence and inspiration across an organization. They're valued for their ability to bring clarity to others' work, and they have to stay keenly aware of their ability to demonstrate empathy, illustrate alignment, and define success for the company and their employees.

Peak-career leaders have to be able to leverage the attributes of their brand like a high-performing utility player. Their brands become synonymous with a role, and then they have to pivot and reset to the next one. This requires the ability to separate brand attributes from roles and repackage them from one position to the next one.

Here are some examples.

From #2 to #1
A common peak-career jump is from one C-Suite role to another. And internally, it can be tricky when someone's brand has become synonymous with their role.

- The Chief Operating Officer moves up to become the CEO.
- The Chief Financial Officer shifts over to become the CEO.
- The General Counsel transitions to the Chief Human Resources Officer.
- The VP Engineering steps up to become the Chief Technology Officer.

Leaders have to think strategically and contribute outside of their own domain. They have to leverage the core attributes of their brands so that others can experience them through a different lens. They can all do it; they're top leaders in their fields and most have the ability to step into several different roles. They just don't always know the timing of the next opportunity, so they aren't ready to shift impressions when they need to.

It wasn't easy for Gus:

Gus was the COO of a new medical center. He'd been in the corporate world for decades but had been tapped to help launch the center's non-profit and was part of the inaugural leadership team for the first two years. When the CEO stepped away, Gus thought he was a shoo-in for the role. But he had a problem…the board didn't agree.

Gus was incredibly smart. He had all of the organization's institutional knowledge and he was more knowledgeable than most of the board on current trends in the industry. The problem was that Gus was not very charismatic and the CEO role was very community-focused. The board saw Gus as "the man behind the scenes," and while he was a valued leader, they just couldn't see him as a strategic leader.

The board brought in an external leader who didn't last nine months. This created an unsettled feeling among employees, so the board positioned Gus as an interim CEO while they began a more thoughtful search. That's when we met Gus. The board felt he needed some help with community visibility as the interim leader, so they reached out to our team.

Once we heard the insights above, we realized that Gus was struggling with a brand issue more than a capabilities issue. He was extremely capable of being a CEO, and the employees believed in him. He just didn't have the backing of the board. Our goal was to help him change brand impressions.

And first, we had to change his perspective. As a strong COO, he had thought his work spoke for itself. He didn't really see the need to share the center's story or build relationships in the community. He thought if he worked harder, the results would convince the board. We knew differently. The board already valued his work as COO; we had to help him reset his brand as a potential CEO.

We knew if Gus could build visibility with external audiences, the board would see his ability to "sell" the vision of the medical center. We helped him develop a storyline that he believed in and felt vested in sharing with groups. We worked on his personal style and ability to draw listeners in with stories of the center's success. We worked through foundational skills until he felt confident in the front of a room. His desire to show hard work didn't go away; he just had a better outlet to illustrate it.

We encouraged Gus to double his visibility in the community. We taught him to tell stories about people, not numbers. And he got really good at it.

The community liked him, and, over time, the board shifted their perspective on him as well. By expanding the view of his brand, Gus helped the board visualize his potential impact in the CEO role.

Gus's story had a great result, but not all misalignments do. And while some of the allure of external candidates is driven by the desire for a new direction for a company, it's also impacted by internal leaders whose roles become their brands.

You can see from Gus' example how important communication was to resetting his brand. He had the opportunity to reset impressions because he was in an interim role. Not every organization has time for interim positions, and not every board is willing to wait to see results. Top executives with aspirations for another leadership role have to leverage communication situations to illustrate their bandwidth and the diversity of their skills.

Lead with What You Learn vs. What You Know

The days of internal promotion for senior leaders are more tempered than they used to be. For senior leadership roles, internal candidates are only selected about one third of the time. And often, the driving force behind that is when a board or leadership team wants to bring in fresh perspectives to stay ahead of the innovation curve, rally a struggling brand, or make a shift in strategy. And while a company can set a new direction quickly, it can't change its employees or its culture quite so fast.

That's where external leaders struggle when onboarding into a new company. New leaders may be directed to think differently, shake things up, and stir the pot. That's why they were hired, and they're eager to get that underway. But the organization may not be. Even though a board bought in to an external candidate, there are other senior leaders already in place. Some may have been internal candidates for the new leader's role. Companies maintain a good deal of loyalty to existing leaders, and this puts a new leader in a tricky spot.

The new leader walks a fine line of balancing the tenured team with a new vision and direction. They will make personnel changes, but, ideally, they need to be able to build trust and camaraderie with some of the existing leaders so that they don't lose all the institutional knowledge. A misstep here creates a slow start and an uphill battle for the new leader.

This happened to both Bert and Jackie:

Bert was a new CEO who came from a consulting background. He took over a large, well-established company, but he wanted to put his own unique brand of leadership on the organization. In his first three months, he dove in with a consultant's mindset to challenge everything.

In every meeting, he asked for more data to back up points, he dug deep with questions, and he presented a counter-perspective. He seemed to be preparing for each discussion with a "why not?" challenge for the presenting leader. He felt energized in a matter of weeks and kept a long list of notes from every meeting. He felt he was being inquisitive and really jumping deep into the business to accelerate his learning.

The existing leadership team soon found him exhausting. Initially, they tried to match his thinking and questions, but in a matter of weeks they grew quiet and withdrawn. Bert took his credentials as an outside expert to heart and, as a result, made the existing leadership team feel inadequate. In short order, the thirst for information created almost daily fire drills across the company as people tried to find specific data points that the previous CEO had never reviewed. Projects were delayed, initiatives were stalled, and morale plummeted as nothing seemed to live up to Bert's expectations.

Bert had a real blind spot to how his leadership style affected people. The turnover at the company spoke volumes. He entered the role with the intention to challenge *strategies*. Instead, he seemed to be challenging *people*. And unintentionally, he pushed half of his top talent right out the door.

Jackie was the antithesis of Bert. She was easy-going and very approachable as a leader. She came from a large company and joined a long-tenured leadership team at her new company. While her brand was more amiable than Bert's, Jackie also struggled to get buy-in for her ideas. She came into her new company as the proverbial "golden girl." She'd had a great deal of success in her former role, and her new company's talent team was excited for her to transfer that success to her new role. But Jackie was quickly seen as an outside expert in a culture where institutional knowledge was the most valued asset.

Every time she brought up a new approach or idea, she received more pushback than she expected from her peer group. She brought in new vendors and went to great lengths to illustrate innovative thinking and new ideas. She just couldn't seem to get traction on her ideas, no matter what she tried. Jackie started lots of new initiatives in her first year, and few of them made it over the finish line. They were her initiatives, and were rarely prioritized by her peers. She felt like she was on an island and hadn't earned the respect of her peers.

No one likes to feel like they're wrong or being challenged. And in different ways, both Bert and Jackie were challenging their teams. Bert made people feel as though they were constantly being tested. Jackie didn't connect new ideas to existing plans, so her peers felt as if they had to give up something to take on something else.

Both are examples of blind spots that should have been intentional strategies in their onboarding. It takes time to learn an organization, identify paths to alignment, and create an intentional plan for influencing an organization. We often tell leaders that onboarding is a two-way process. You're not just onboarding yourself; you're onboarding everyone else as well. Most leaders are coached on the importance of listening for the first hundred days. We put intention behind the listening.

The time should be focused on more than just connecting with employees. It's about tracking what you're hearing and what you're not hearing. Your notes aren't just to capture knowledge. You're gathering input that should be used as proof points of what you heard and a starting point for what you'd like to do.

It would have helped Jackie to connect her ideas to her peers' priorities. She needed to align new ideas to their desired outcomes. She knew that the culture valued tenure, and she would have had more success in her first year if she attached to others' plans rather than trying to position her ideas on their own.

Bert actually was taking notes, but he was so eager to quench his own thirst for knowledge that he ran well ahead of his team. He missed the obvious signs of moving too fast and shut down his ability to get feedback.

Filling Big Shoes

When a seasoned, well-liked leader leaves on a high note, the person coming behind them has their work cut out for them. The expectations are unrealistic, and the comparisons are unavoidable. And when a well-liked leader is taken out by a board unexpectedly, that creates its own set of challenges for an incoming leader.

And that's what DeAndra walked into in her first CEO role:

DeAndra was from New Orleans, and she was named the CEO of a large manufacturing company located in a small Midwest town. The company was a family-owned business and probably employed close to 25% of the town. The former CEO, Jim, had been there nearly thirty years, and

135

his employees adored him. He'd been very loyal to them and their families for over a decade, and no one was happy to hear that he'd been removed. From his senior leadership team down to the front-line workers, the immediate focus of hostility became DeAndra.

DeAndra knew all of this going in to the role. She thought she was prepared for it, but as her upcoming move got closer and closer, she began to feel less certain. She was going to be moving to this town, living next door to her managers, and going to the grocery store with the whole company. She knew that the family had voted to bring in an outsider to run the company. Jim had been a great leader, but he wasn't getting the company to the next level. The family wanted to keep their reasons confidential, and so they had said little about the change.

DeAndra had enormous shoes to fill, and she didn't think she would ever live up to Jim's legacy. She was never going to be the same kind of leader, and trying to be like him was only going to invite more comparisons. So we worked to be intentional about the brand DeAndra wanted to put forward.

We knew that people needed to get to know her and begin to like her as person before they accepted her as the leader, so we helped her think about informal ways to share herself and her experiences. She talked about her family and her early life. She talked about "learning the Midwest" to make her newness something fun that her employees could enjoy about her. It gave them an easy way to connect with her and begin to see her more as a person than as an unknown boss.

Vulnerability is something we'll address more in the following sections. But in terms of a leader's brand, it's a crucial piece of moving beyond a former leader's shadow. Most people want to do the opposite. They're worried that by sharing more of themselves, they will only heighten key differences and spotlight gaps. It might...but that's the point. You aren't your predecessor, and you can't stop people from making comparisons. The key to minimizing those comparisons is to stand up a very different brand that suggests a different experience to employees.

As a leader, you need to define your own brand of leadership. In DeAndra's case, her strategy of openness allowed others to see her as a very different leader. Different, but a leader nonetheless. And by leaning in to the difference in her style rather than trying to mirror or replace Jim, DeAndra was able to establish her own brand of leadership and defuse a skeptical employee base.

Section III

The Art of the Interview

17

Disrupted!...Again

I will never forget the worst interview I've ever had.
After making it through numerous rounds of personality
interviews, assessments, and case studies, I received the
following email at 6:00 p.m. on Friday:

"Hi Hurst. Enjoyed our conversation yesterday. We'd like to
invite you to our final round of interviews in our New York
offices next week. Can you fly in on Monday?"

I had been to New York several times, but never for an
interview. I booked a *very* expensive flight that night over
a celebratory Shiner beer and found a friend to watch my
dog. I dug out my best suit over the weekend and was so
excited about the company and opportunity that I somehow
got to the Houston airport three hours early for a
7:00 a.m. flight.

I felt confident and *relevant* as my cab creeped through
Manhattan and arrived at the company's office half an
hour early. I was ready to dazzle my interviewers with the
same energy and elevator pitch I'd brought to my virtual
interviews. And then...I remember waiting.

I probably waited close to two hours in their lobby before a receptionist finally brought me back to a small conference room and offered a brief apology for the delay. The company had been responding to a fire drill that morning, but all of my interviews would still happen – they would just be combined. This meant that instead of five one-to-one interviews, I would have two, two-to-one meetings and then one solo meeting with HR. I said that this was no problem and that I completely understood. I shook hands with the first two leaders and sat down, ready to answer any and all of their questions.

And then one of the interviewers threw me a curveball.

"So, your experience is mostly analytics-based," he said. "You're really more of an analyst than a consultant."

That was not a question I had been asked at any point in the interview process, and it felt a little hostile. I don't actually remember what I said in response, but I do remember immediately feeling like I was put on the defensive, seemingly out of the blue. I must not have pivoted very well, because the interviewer followed up with a brief description of the role and left the floor open for me to make a case for myself. The other interviewer asked two questions about previous roles on my resume, and then they both left after about fifteen minutes.

I'd been in enough interviews to know that that one had not gone well. But I had a second chance with the next group, so I shook my head clear and used the time I had before the next mini panel to think through how I would answer the analyst vs. consultant question if I was asked again. I had a pretty good answer ready when the second interview got underway.

And as it did, one of the second panelists said, "So, I see a lot of writing experience on your resume. Do you know that this role has a heavy analytics component to it?"

Now I was thoroughly confused. I had just been knocked one way by the first panelist and then the second came back from the other direction, apparently contradicting the first leader's description of the job. This question was much more in my wheelhouse, as I had plenty of analytics experience. It was why I was so interested in the role to begin with!

But this leader seemed fixated on my writing experience, and her line of questioning seemed so at odds with the first group that I'm sure I must have botched that interview as well. I remember a lot of circular discussion and a growing sense of frustration, because the interviewer didn't seem to grasp the experience I knew I had that was right on the paper in front of her.

I left New York City disappointed and confused. I received a polite (but short) rejection two days later informing me that "while I was not a fit for this role, they would keep my resume on hand in case my skill set fit a future need."

I've thought about those interviews a lot over the years. And looking back, I can see where the disconnects occurred.

I was a good fit for that role, and I knew it. I think the first three people who interviewed me virtually for the position thought so as well. In fact, I was probably far too confident that I'd already won the role when I walked into their office. I felt connected through those first virtual interviews and aligned to the role, so I thought I was ready to answer any questions the next interviewers might ask me. The role was a perfect fit to anyone who knew me.

And that was the crux of the problem. *I* knew me, and *I* knew that I was a great fit…but the leaders who interviewed me in-person didn't. I had had an easy rapport with the talent-acquisition team, and they had told me multiple times that I was a great fit for what they were looking for. And I had assumed that that feedback was shared up the interview chain.

- "I really like Hurst! He's got a great background for what we're looking for."
- "I spent more than an hour with him. He understands our business and nailed our case study!"
- "Seems like a great culture fit. I think he's really interested in the role!"

I'll never know if that feedback was ever shared, and in the end, it didn't matter. What did matter was that I interviewed with this company on a bad day. The receptionist told me that when she explained that they were dealing with a fire drill, and I'm sure those leaders were deep in that problem when she reminded them that I was in town to interview. At best, I was interviewing with a distracted audience, and at worst, I was dealing with an audience that was stressed, flustered, and not interested in me that day.

Most likely, my in-person interviewers forgot anything their recruiting team told them during their hectic morning.

That may sound like an unfortunate circumstance, but it's a common one. These leaders weren't disinterested, but they *were* distracted. And in looking for a way to get focused on the interview, they looked for what they knew about me – what was printed on my resume. And as you heard, two leaders interpreted my resume very differently!

At the time, I felt this was remarkably unfair. I had prepared for the interviews, and it was clear that those leaders had not. But that was not what caused me to stumble in the interview. The disconnect was that, while I was prepared to react to questions about myself, I had not taken the time to think through how I wanted to position myself.

This is the difference between being **a reactive interviewee** vs. **a proactive interviewee**. And it's a common mistake people make during an interview process. We know our accomplishments, and we've taken time to put together a chronological resume that showcases our experience, but then we take a backseat in the interview process and wait to be asked questions. We put the responsibility on the interviewer to bring our experience to life.

Most of us are reactive. And as you saw above in my story, my reaction was not good when the interviewers' questions caught me off-guard.

Imagine how the conversation might have shifted if I had been more proactive. What if I'd been prepared with central themes about my experiences? For example, if I had been prepared to showcase my adaptability, the interview might have gone more like this:

Interviewer: "So, your experience is mostly analytics-based. You're really more of an analyst than a consultant."

Me: "Well, it's interesting you mention that. Analytics is how I got started at Company B, but my role quickly shifted within the first month when the company's needs changed and my manager needed an associate to fill an account role. I found myself in a much more client-facing role almost overnight. That's really where I discovered my passion for client-facing interaction. And it's actually why I became interested in this consulting role…"

Or, if I wanted to showcase my critical thinking skills with the second panelist:

Interviewer: "So, I see a lot of writing experience on your resume. Do you know that this role has a heavy analytics component to it?"

Me: "Yes, and it's why I'm really excited to blend the two skill sets in this opportunity. Most of my writing experience was at Company A, where I worked on corporate plans and long-term strategies. I developed a strong analytics background working on Company C's latest R&D efforts. But what I'm most interested in is the interaction of the two, when a depth in analytics can strengthen insights shared in recommendations to clients."

The difference you hear in both of these examples is an interviewee who has a clear message they want to convey about consulting experience and analytics experience blending together. They know what they've done and, most importantly, they know how to position their experiences.

Both examples I shared in these interview re-dos came from the same resume. But a proactive and compelling interviewee knows how to position their experiences to keep an interviewer focused on clear themes and takeaways.

The trends of disruption will reach beyond impressions and ultimately create movement in your career. And as a result, the interviewing experience will become a more frequent event. Your career may become a winding road instead of a single-lane highway. And it stands to reason that, to prepare for more interviews and different roles, you need to know how companies recruit talent and what you can do to take charge of your story in every interview.

18

Personal Resets

So, about career resets.

How should you think about them? As we discussed in Chapters 2 and 3, disruption can be a personal choice or a corporate mandate. How you reset from disruption is fully a choice.

In an early career, we often see impatience as a reason for reset. The early career stage is that time in life where people are eager for opportunity and impatient to get it. The grass always seems greener at another company…and sometimes it is. Getting and accelerating opportunities is more about the demands of the company than those of the individual. And early career individuals can get frustrated by that. We talked about this earlier in the book. Most early career movement is self-inflicted or self-motivated. As you explore reset options at this stage, it isn't that complicated to transition to a new job and a new location. It just takes time and effort to look for opportunities and put yourself forward for them.

In mid-career, reset is a balance of corporate disruption and corporate recruitment. As managers and their brands become known and valued, many are recruited to new roles and new companies. Others still seek opportunities themselves. The process gets a little more complicated as mid-career managers need more to make a reset worth it, from an expanded compensation plan to expanded ownership and responsibility.

If mid-career managers have been disrupted by a company, they often leave with a nice severance package, which gives them time to think over their reset step. Changing companies can be more complicated for mid-career employees, as by mid-career people are often more settled in communities with families or interests that have developed outside their jobs. Interviewing involves multiple steps and establishing impressions with multiple people. Even when mid-career employees reset within their existing companies, they'll have to position themselves with a broader audience.

And by peak career, search firms and recruiters lead the process. The recruiters are an added lens of connection and a valued filter to companies. Recruiters watch industries, and they track candidates. A peak-career move is a big move for all involved. As we mentioned in the discussion of brands in Chapter 8, companies plan to leverage the brand of a leadership candidate either as a new entity or a known entity. Contracts, signing bonuses, stock options, relocations, and benefits are all a part of the discussion. It may take a few years for a peak-career leader to land a reset opportunity. Or it may take months for an executive recruiter to convince a high-profile leader to move for another chapter. These are big stakes moves with big expectations and big rewards.

Across all of the reset options, the common denominator is the interview. Some seasoned leaders are considered real pros at interviewing, but no one likes it. And across all three career phases above, most people view the interview as a necessary part of a reset opportunity.

In the best of circumstances, interviews are stressful. In the worst, interviews can cause a lot of self-doubt and anxiety. But the truth is, you need to get good at interviewing. Whether you're disrupted by a company shift or you choose to explore a different role or a different culture at a new company, interviews are an integral part of getting to the next opportunity.

For a single position, there are usually six to ten people who make it through the application process and begin a series of interviews. Only two to three of those will go into a final round of interviews…and only one will get an offer. And that means that an interview is far more likely to be unsuccessful than successful.

Even if you have great presence and feel well-qualified for a role, interviews can still go sideways. Remember Hurst's example in the last chapter: what started out great, deteriorated very quickly. And maybe that's because the biggest challenge of interviewing is that the interview process is a step most people don't understand as well as they should. That's why we gathered insights from talent-acquisition leaders to add corporate perspective on the reset process.

19

Corporate Priorities–
Insights from Talent Acquisition

We surveyed hundreds of talent-acquisition and recruitment leaders, asking them questions about trends in recruiting and looking for similarities and differences between what talent acquisition is doing to bring in new talent and what talent development is doing to develop skills of internal talent.

Close to 90% of talent-acquisition leaders and talent-development leaders said that you should understand your personal brand, know your strengths and skills, and understand how they fit in your career. They agreed that individuals must position themselves for career advancement and promotion opportunities, and only 23% of the acquisition leaders thought their companies took ownership for getting people promotion-ready. You may remember that the talent development perspective was even less, at 10%.

So, the two groups who have a lot of influence in your growth and opportunities within an organization are saying that *you* have to take responsibility for it.

But they represent two different perspectives when it comes to jobs within a company. The talent-development team is working under the direction of company goals and strategy to *anticipate* what a company will need. The talent-acquisition team is working to fill the needs *right now*.

Talent acquisition is often a team whose responsibilities are a little vague to most employees. Once you join a company, you may not pay much attention to what they're doing. After all, they're in charge of hiring people and you've already been hired. But there's a little more to their function. Talent acquisition supports a company's strategy by ensuring they have the right people in the right roles at the right time. And this means that the fast-paced shifts within a company put an acquisition or recruitment team under pressure to find the talent they need.

Here's how they define their focus:

- Acquiring high-quality candidates who offer skills needed for current roles
- Building a diverse talent pool to meet current and future business needs
- Assessing current in-house skills to determine future skills and roles needed
- Identifying talented employees within the company to groom for promotion

So, talent acquisition has a view of both external and internal talent. And they have the most comprehensive view of the two groups to compare.

When we shared talent-development insights in Chapter 3, you heard urgency in how the development leaders think about developing internal talent. And that urgency only increases for talent-acquisition teams. The talent-acquisition survey participants define top challenges as competition for top talent and a shortage of qualified talent. Both perspectives illustrate the rapid pace of change and the choices companies are making in order to deliver on it.

As we mentioned with talent development, it takes time to teach employees new skills and, in a competitive marketplace with product rushes and aggressive deadlines, it's not always a viable solution to retrain an entire function of a business or invest in an internal candidate.

That's why the top reason for selecting external candidates rather than internal ones is the need for a new skill or expertise (65%). And it just makes you wonder, was the skill truly missing within the company or was the skill just not promoted as part of an internal brand? Sometimes, there's no question that a new skill or expertise is being added. But there are many times that skills were just not recognized. And here's how we know.

When we asked talent acquisition what most people can't do well in an interview, they say it's the ability to illustrate accomplishments.

"Some of the best candidates we interview in terms of relative experience, education, and skill set are not always the best at being able to tell their story. And this can be a real impediment when you're trying to convince me to hire you! The one skill that I recommend candidates develop to help them land a job or launch a career is to become an exceptional storyteller. Specifically, a teller of your own story."

We couldn't ask for a better proof point for the importance of a career story! Your accomplishments and experiences are like a doorjamb for a job position. They are what will get you the first-round interview, but no matter how much of a rock star your resume says you are, the way you communicate your accomplishments and tell your story is what gets you to the next round.

And if you agree with the trends and insights that we're sharing, then disruption will continue whether you put it into play or your company does. You're going to be a candidate multiple times. You'll go through more interviews – and meet more talent-acquisition people – than you ever thought you would. And there's no one in the company who knows more about interview expectations and pitfalls than the talent-acquisition group.

They shared expectations from the candidates' perspective and then their own. Here's what candidates are looking for today:

- A deeper understanding of the opportunity and how it complements their career goals
- An opportunity to have an impact
- A "day in the life" of the position and a chance to meet real people doing the job
- More insights and information about the person they will be working for
- Flexibility to work remotely

Overall, candidates want to be coached through the application process and they want closure on the process.

Companies are fast to open roles but not always as fast to make decisions. A new trend that executive search firms are experiencing with top leadership candidates is that the longer process loses candidates. People aren't as willing to wait to work through multiple steps. Once the interview process is put in motion, candidates want the process to move along.

We also asked talent acquisition what they're looking for in candidates and what makes a candidate memorable to them. They said that sharing impactful accomplishments (80%), having great communication skills (78%), and asking relevant questions (75%) are what make a candidate memorable.

We agree! It's the ability to shape your brand across the phases of your career and the ability to communicate it in a confident and compelling manner that matters most.
In fact, it isn't just the ability to talk about accomplishments that matters, but the ability to connect those accomplishments to your key themes and attributes. Doesn't that sound like the brand map we discussed in Chapter 6?

We also asked talent acquisitions what the toughest roles to fill are. While eight of the top ten roles are technology roles, the reason isn't always competition for talent. Talent leaders say that technical candidates don't have the ability to show their work or easily explain with examples. And salespeople tend to over-talk, trying to sell their personalities rather than their results.

Talent acquisition leaders agree on the most critical skills needed within an organization. You've seen this chart before, and it aligns closely to the insights from talent development. In fact, both groups agree these are the critical and most transferrable skills. That means that if you're known for these attributes, you're a great candidate to leverage in many different roles. We wouldn't be surprised if this is a common discussion point and measurement used in talent reviews.

Copy this list and put it next to that brand map. This tells you what you need to develop and illustrate across your career experience.

Talent Acquisition vs. Talent Development
Top Critical Skills

TALENT ACQUISITION	TALENT DEVELOPMENT
1 Problem-solving & Critical Thinking	1 Communication & Influence
2 Collaborative & Cooperative	2 Agility During Change & Uncertainty
3 Communication & Influence	3 Problem-solving & Critical Thinking

Here's the tough news about all these insights. Talent acquisition acknowledges that companies look outside for skills when they don't have them internally. But we believe internal teams can't always see the skills because they aren't touching the entire workforce. Remember how narrowly the talent-development group defined their focus? You should think about whether you have a skill gap or a brand gap. There's a difference.

When an opportunity comes down to an internal candidate vs. an external one, as long as the skill sets are equal, the internal brand should have the home-court advantage. But this often isn't the case. The external candidate starts with a clean slate; every interview sets first impressions. This means that the external candidate often does a better job of positioning a brand. That's good news if you're moving to a new company, but if you're trying to get promoted within a company, it means you can't wait for an interview to position your brand internally. This validates everything we called out in the first half of this book. You have to constantly be working to position your brand so that you're on the radar for opportunities.

And we can help you do that. Now that you understand the expectations, let's explore the tools that help you communicate about yourself, not just in an interview, but throughout your career.

There's an art and a science to how to talk about yourself, and it involves a little storytelling prowess.

20

A Step Back or a Step Ahead

You might've found yourself recalling some of your own interviewing pitfalls in the previous three chapters, or you might have been realizing just how lucky you've been to escape them so far. Regardless of your own history with interviewing to date, you can see that it's the critical step to resetting and that it condenses all the elements of impressions and assumptions down to a matter of weeks and a group of a few key people.

In order to feel that you can work through disruption and continue to advance your career through any of the phases, you have to be able to interview well. That may not be welcome news as you think about your own experience. If you picked up this book because you were disrupted by a company's shift in direction, you may be working through feelings of resentment, disappointment, and a little self-doubt.

Or if you got interested in the topic because you want to shift gears, you may be feeling excited, confident, and on top of your game because you know your skills are in high demand. Both perspectives show up during job opportunities because feelings and emotions come through around questions about roles. And talent acquisition leaders say it's never a good idea to talk negatively about former employers!

It takes mental focus to get ready for a new opportunity. No matter why you're resetting, you need to see the next step as a forward step and not a back step. This can be hard to do. As companies reset their plans or just adjust their expenses, many valued and tenured employees are getting red slips and "early retirement" offers. It isn't personal, but it sure *feels* personal. Your next opportunity may mean a cut in salary, may be a change in title, or may look nothing like the one you left behind. You may need to look at roles with a little less ego and a little more runway in terms of what a role could become. Or you may take advantage of a severance package and look very broadly at a totally different direction. This has become very common for peak-career layoffs.

We meet people at both extremes of reset: those who are deflated by a layoff and those who are energized by an opportunity. And you can literally see the difference in someone who is being dragged into the process and someone who is jumping in with both feet. Your confidence needs to be restored before you begin the interview process. Disruption and resets are going to happen. But you want to feel prepared to not only survive the search for a new opportunity, but to jump in wholeheartedly.

So assume you've made it to the interview round. Your resume seemed to do the trick, and you're set to begin a series of interviews. The interviewers are handed six to ten resumes, whether by an internal recruiter or an external search firm. This group of candidates have "passed the test" in terms of capability and experience, so the interviewers have a group of people who have been determined to be a lot alike. Your goal in the interviews is to make your brand stand apart. When the recruiter circles back, what will an interviewer say about you? They met seven or more people. Do they remember much about you?

They will...*if* you've mastered the skill of talking about yourself. You've seen in previous chapters what can happen in an interview when you relinquish control of the conversation to an interviewer. But the way you talk about yourself goes far beyond just the interview. How you talk about yourself and your journey forms the second integral piece of your professional development. You can be the smartest, most accomplished person in the room, but if you can't position your experience and your expertise in a way that connects to a new opportunity, you'll limit your next steps without even realizing it.

While we talked about the importance of impressions in the first half of this book, now it's time to focus on how you talk about yourself in the moments when you have an opportunity to put your brand forward. We'll start with the interview because there's no other communication format that's more centered around disruption. But ultimately, we'll coach you to think through your career story and leverage your personal stories and experiences in many different ways.

And we'll start with expectations across career levels so you can see that, while the tools remain the same, the expectations are different, just as they were with brand.

21

Interview Expectations Across a Career

Just like we did in Section I, we'll focus on distinctions around expectations across our three different levels: Early Career, Mid-Career and Peak Career.

The critical skills called out by talent-acquisition leaders were: Problem-Solving & Critical Thinking, Collaborative & Cooperative, and Communication & Influence. These skills seem to be universal priorities across all roles, as talent leaders are focused on finding people who are disciplined thinkers, adaptable learners and collaborators, and, ultimately, strong communicators who can be key influencers within an organization. But the expectations for how those skills are exemplified intensify as a career progresses.

Let's take a closer look.

Early Career

When we talked about building your early career brand back in Chapter 5, the conversation was about building visibility and value across an organization. Visibility is a strategy that often gets you to an interview, but the interview itself will lean heavily on value. How do you illustrate value across the three priorities called out as critical skills?

To illustrate critical thinking and problem-solving, you'll want to communicate a broader impact for the problem that you were a part of solving or use examples of projects and assignments where you were involved from beginning to end. Focus on sharing examples from the business perspective rather than your specific role. This helps an interviewer see that you understood the broader application of your work. Talk about measurable business outcomes from projects rather than just completed steps of your tasks.

For example, if you worked on a project that automated customer-service requests and your job was to build the gateway that connected the service requests to technicians, don't just tell the recruiter your role in the project.

"Last year, I worked on a project to automate our online service requests. I worked on the automation step that routed service requests to technicians and reduced the customers' entry time by 60%."

Instead, attach your initiative to the broader business objective, like this:

"Last year, I worked on a nine-month project to automate our customer-service requests. It involved twelve steps that linked online service requests to service technicians. It was designed to simplify the customer experience and create transparency in our technicians' workload. I worked on the step that routed service requests to technicians and reduced the customers' entry time by 60%. In fact, three months into the new process, we realized that we had improved the technicians' workload by 30% because we had streamlined the service offerings and matched tickets to the most qualified technicians. By the end of the year, our company's online service went from being rated 'Poor' by our customers to being one of our top three best-reviewed attributes."

Your ability to collaborate will come through if you include colleagues in your examples or share insights on how you learned or adapted skills from others. Share examples of times that you proactively sought guidance and input. As you think through your career experiences, be sure that the ability to work with and influence others comes through.

Depending on your career path to date, you may also need to address concerns about unintentional patterns that show up in your experience or seem to be stereotypes of an early career employee. While job-hopping has become more culturally acceptable over time, there are reservations that surround it from a company's perspective if investment and training still remain. To a recruiter, too many roles in too few years reads as someone who is unattached or uninterested. Are you going to leave when things don't go your way? Or are you unsure of who you are and what you want?

If you've changed jobs three times in five years, first impressions may be that you're someone who is drifting and hasn't yet learned how to build a marketable skill set. But imagine how much more compelling a candidate you would be if you could flip that assumption on its head!

The job-hopping itself is not the issue, so long as you can justify the career intentions behind each stop. Are you working toward developing a new proficiency that your first two companies did not have? Have you developed cross-functional expertise to move you toward the role you're really passionate about? When we think about an early career professional who can justify their own career moves and paint a narrative of intent behind their movements, the impressions shift from perceiving that person as someone who is drifting to someone who has passion and direction.

Mid-Career

In your mid-career, you build a brand by focusing on clarity and influence. By the time you reach an interview and have the opportunity to highlight your brand, you'll quickly see that communication has become a distinguishing factor. Chances are that you've already noticed the wide discrepancy of managers at this career level. Some seem to be rising stars who are catapulted into leadership positions almost overnight, and others appear stuck below a glass ceiling that they can't seem to break through.

A recruiter may look past some gaps in clarity and communication if an early career candidate has the specific skill set they need, but they expect mid-career candidates to be good at illustrating their experience. And you may remember from Chapter 19 that they said that most candidates aren't. Most people assume their resume will do the talking for them. They've built a compelling list of achievements and expect that experience to speak for itself.

But that's a disconnect with most talent teams. They're not looking for a simple list of successes and references. That's just to get the process started. What companies are looking for out of a mid-career manager is whether they can back up their experiences with how they talk about themselves. You might have the strongest background in operational finance or the longest tenure managing legal compliance among candidates, but if you can't articulate the kind of manager you are or what is unique about your approach to typical challenges the company may face, you're missing a talent team's main interest.

They don't want you to just talk about your experience. They expect you to be able to tell them why those experiences make you the best candidate for the role. As you move higher up in any organization, the emphasis becomes less on what you've achieved to date, and more about how those experiences have positioned you to be successful tomorrow.

Chances are your resume may highlight some poor career steps or times when you seemed to get stuck in one position. Recruiters look for trends and themes across paths. You should know what yours are. Don't try to hide them; be prepared to explain them. There isn't a right answer or a reason to dodge the question, but it's important to be able to explain a stall in advancement confidently. When you get caught by surprise or seem embarrassed by a stall, an interviewer will assume there's more to the story.

You should know the difference between managing people and leading people, and you should be able to illustrate that difference to an interviewer. You should be able to illustrate critical thinking through your ability to second-guess a current approach or rethink a decision and move in a different direction. Don't just share the results, be sure that your examples highlight the broader thinking that goes into problem-solving before reaching solutions. You need to come across as someone who can work across blurred lines and who doesn't need clear-cut direction. And while clarity will show up in your ability to communicate during the interview, influence goes hand in hand with collaboration. Be sure "I" is no longer the way you communicate about results and projects. "We" suggests someone who has internalized the way they work and cooperate with others.

Peak Career

Expectations shift again as you interview for peak-career roles. In the brand discussion, we called out authenticity and repeatability as attributes that leaders develop in order to become candidates for senior leadership.

When seeking a senior leader, a company is not just looking for someone who employees will relate to, they're looking for someone who can bang the war drum and energize teams of hundreds to thousands. Your brand becomes synonymous with the company's brand, and you have to embody the direction and strategy of the organization.

Back in Chapter 8, we told you that employees want a leader who is Hercules, Mother Teresa, and Braveheart all rolled into one. And those expectations certainly don't change in what a talent team is looking for. Companies are looking for that X factor in a leader that employees will recognize and latch on to. It's not enough just to be authentic as a leader; you also have to be able to motivate an organization.

Beyond sales numbers and market growth, can you energize employees to not only meet their yearly goals, but to *want* to go beyond expectations and innovate for the consumer? That's the measure of a great peak-career professional and what takes you from being a competent leader to a compelling one.

How will recruiters assess all of that in a few meetings? They say they can spot the X factor in less than an hour. But they also say that their job is to help the company find the right fit. So, while the ability to communicate and influence is all about you, they're most interested in how well you translate your experience to the company at hand. Think forward, not back. Use your experience to position questions and insights about the next step for the potential company. Spend less time on what you've done and more time on what's possible in this opportunity. Recruiters expect peak-career candidates to illustrate their understanding of a company and an industry through insightful questions and potential strategies that a new leader would take with a company.

If you pass the recruiter stage, you should begin thinking about early steps you would take if given the position. What would you need to know more about? How much can you learn on your own to get to know the company? Can you bring one fresh idea to the leadership team you meet during the interview? Can you illustrate respect and interest for (and position broad thinking around) where they're going? Can you step into the role just enough that they get a glimpse of what you would do if you joined the team the next week?

Senior-level positions are seats of power. Most Boards and other senior leaders start from a place of trust and comfort. Will they be comfortable with you? Will they be able to trust you? This sounds like a great advantage for an internal candidate, and yet internal candidates only move to top jobs 30–40% of the time. In Chapter 19, recruiters said that they go outside of their organizations for new thinking. This reinforces how important it is to illustrate strategic thinking in current roles and to make sure your brand doesn't get pigeonholed in a company.

At the root of comfort and trust is uncovering missteps. Senior-level positions carry high visibility, which comes with risk around anyone's brand. Companies dig deep to understand missteps, and they would be doubtful of a candidate who doesn't have them. You should be prepared to talk through bad decisions and career setbacks. If you've been fired, don't be defensive. Add both perspectives to your account of the situation. If you didn't get along with a Board, take responsibility for not making it work. You have to balance confidence with humility and acknowledge how you could have improved a situation.

You can expect to be asked about servant leadership. Today's peak-career candidates have to illustrate that employees come first and that the success of every employee matters to you. You have to show cross-functional understanding, collaboration, and cooperation. You need to illustrate investment in driving an entire organization forward, not just your own division. Does it matter to you as the Chief Sales Officer that the Engineering Team is successful? Do you think with a "one company" perspective? Can you illustrate that your mindset is already there, or will you have to learn this?

The ability to communicate only intensifies as your opportunities progress. If you can communicate a compelling narrative that illustrates your career journey and your intentions across that journey, you'll be able to adapt your experiences to position yourself as a compelling candidate. And the interview process is the moment it all comes together.

22

Resumes vs. Conversations

The last time you interviewed, do you remember much about the interviewer(s)? Most recruiters say managers and leaders aren't terrific at preparing to interview someone. While the search team can give them guidance and notes on candidates, most managers don't give the interview itself a lot of thought in advance. Some have "standard" questions they like to ask to get to know someone, but most count on picking up a resume to guide the interview.

A resume is a timeline. And when an interviewer relies on your resume to guide discussion, they're likely to interview you in one of two ways: 1) chronologically from one role to the next or 2) sporadically from one company to another, focused on roles that interest them. Either way, the presentation of your brand becomes a series of data points that may or may not connect to the ideas the interviewer has of the role. After a series of interviews with a series of candidates, it often comes down to who had the right answer for the right question. And this can be left too much to chance with an interviewer who didn't give a lot of thought to the discussion and the time that you'll spend together.

Most interviewees get led into this reactive discussion. They answer a linear or disconnected list of questions and rarely have a plan for how the data points add up to an overarching story of their careers. Even in an interview process that's case-study-heavy, the way you position yourself and your skill set can determine the course of the conversation. We often say that a resume is designed to organize information, but we believe you need a tool that helps you influence a conversation. This is a different document…a messaging document. A messaging document is a different way of pulling all the data points of a career into central themes that help someone see your skills as transferrable from one role to another.

Remember Chapter 19? Talent acquisition called out their most critical skills and attributes: problem-solving and critical thinking, collaborative and cooperative, and communication and influence. Unless there has been an organized plan for interviews, an interviewer isn't likely to search for your qualifications along those lines. But you can organize qualifications as key themes, and you can think about how those themes illustrate these attributes. You can think through the attributes that best describe your skills, and you can organize your experiences under each theme to illustrate your skills. You can proactively plan for the themes that you want to define you in the conversation. It may not change the interviewers' initial questions, but it can totally shift your responses. It gives you a better sense of how to connect skills rather than getting pigeonholed, like we saw happen in Chapter 17.

"So…you're really more of an analyst than a consultant." That line of questioning had felt like a challenge and quickly threw Hurst back on his heals. But if he had developed a messaging document to organize his experience around key themes, he would have been more successful at connecting data to his analyst experience. In fact, he would have seen an opportunity to position his combination of both skills as a differentiating concept.

If Hurst had used the alternative answers we discussed in Chapter 17, then in all likelihood the conversation would then shift to the value of both perspectives. And if Hurst was well-prepared to build out that theme, the interviewer would take an interest in it and the conversation would shift to proof points and illustrations of how the two skill sets work together.

That kind of flexibility comes from having a prepared messaging document. It's the difference between a reactive interviewee who leaves impressions and key points up to the interviewer vs. a proactive interviewee who has put thought and planning into the key themes they want to get across. The resume is designed for an interviewer. Our messaging document is designed for the interviewee. By streamlining your key points into central themes, you can lead an interviewer to your desired impressions and takeaways. And in the next chapter, we'll show you how to create that document.

23

The Messaging Document

Based on the fast pace of change in companies and all the reasons we've given you for disruption, you should have a resume that's up to date and ready to share. You will meet people throughout your career who will ask for a resume to keep you in mind, or maybe you'll pique someone's interest at an industry event and they'll reach out a week later with an opportunity. The first step in most new opportunities is "send me your resume." This request catches many people unprepared because they haven't looked at their resumes in years. Your first step to reset is to stay ready!

We fine-tune a lot of resumes at SW&A, and our work focuses on wording, clarity, and examples. We help people tighten descriptions and think about the overall presentation of their career paths. But when we get someone ready for an interview, we shift our focus to their messaging document. It's our way of bringing focus and memorability to the conversation itself.

Content always comes back to organizing by threes. Listeners find it easy to remember things in threes, and so do interviewers. Your goal is to identify three themes in your career that best align with a job description or with what you're looking for in a role. If you're looking for similar roles, the themes may stay consistent from one interview to the next. If you're looking at a variety of opportunities, you could develop a different messaging document for each role.

Under each theme, we align examples of your experience with stories that illustrate the experience. We want to help you steer the conversation to those themes and repeat the themes so that the conversation goes deeper into your expertise instead of jumping from one topic to the next.

This is very similar to how we prepare people for media interviews. A journalist has a prepared list of questions. They aren't always related to each other. If an interviewee allows the journalist to follow a list of questions, it's hard to really make messages stick. The interview becomes just a list of responses that follow questions, and the power of the storyline is left with the journalist. The same idea applies in a job interview. If the interviewee doesn't come back to key themes and messages, the themes and messages may not stick or even be heard at all.

In our workshops, we often describe this as turning a linear interview into a more connected conversation.

Here's our model:

STATEMENT/GOAL: This is the headline statement from your resume.

SKILL SET #1: Skill 1	SKILL SET #2: Skill 2	SKILL SET #3: Skill 3
EXAMPLES	**EXAMPLES**	**EXAMPLES**
1. Skill set example 1	**1.** Skill set example 1	**1.** Skill set example 1
2. Skill set example 2	**2.** Skill set example 2	**2.** Skill set example 2
3. Skill set example 3	**3.** Skill set example 3	**3.** Skill set example 3
STORY	**STORY**	**STORY**
• **Supporting Story 1**	• **Supporting Story 2**	• **Supporting Story 3**

To understand the relationship between resumes and messaging documents, we've created examples to support all three phases of a career.

Our examples are from real experiences, but the people and companies are fictitious and developed as illustrations only. They'll provide easy examples to help you consider your resume and the themes you should pull out of it.

Early Career: Victoria Pfluger

Victoria is very early career. She is a soon-to-be college graduate seeking a consulting role. She has great intern experience and strong grades for consideration. So will hundreds of other applicants from hundreds of other universities. Take a look at her resume and then move on to the messaging document.

Victoria Pfluger

jpluger18@school.edu | 123-456-7890 | 55 Main Street, College Town, USA

A financial analyst with modeling expertise and the ability to inspire teamwork and lead peer groups.

Education

Northern Illinois University, DeKalb, IL   May 2021

English Major, Business Minor | GPA: 3.8 | President's Honor Roll

Relevant Coursework
Microeconomics, Issues in Financial Reporting I, Financial Accounting, Business Leadership, Business Communications, Principles of Economics, Single Variable Calculus 1 & 2, Honors Shakespeare, West African Comparative Literature

West Grove High School, Hometown, ST   May 2017

GPA: 93/100

Work Experience

Senior Analyst | Premier Global Consulting, Remote Internship   June 2020–August 2020

Developed financial models (DCF) used for share price valuation, researched comparable companies, and pitched stocks within the real estate and energy sectors

Tax Intern | Wilson, Lalter & Solomon, PA, Chicago, IL   June 2019–August 2019

Prepared federal, state, and local tax returns with complete workpapers for individuals, partnerships, S-corps and trusts using XYZ tax software
Prepared analysis for asset allocation updates for client portfolios

Intern | Mid-West Construction Services, Austin, TX   June 2018–August 2018

Analyzed company investments and prepared company financial statements

Extracurricular Activities and Volunteer Service

Advisor | Peer Academic Advisors   February 2020–Present

Direct students to academic planning resources for graduation requirements and pre-professional tracks

Ambassador | Student Orientation Program   August 2018–Present

Introduce and aide transition of students from high school

Co-President | Laugh Guild, Improv Comedy Club   August 2017–Present

Manage club finances and plan fundraisers
Compete in various comedy tournaments and participate in regular performances

Team Captain | Club Water Polo Team   August 2017–Present

Serve as team captain and goalkeeper for school club team

Awards/Certificates

Outstanding Delegate, Model United Nations   March 2020

Received individual recognition and award for leading Belgian delegation

Youngston English Department Book Award   2020

Scholarship to fund post-graduate research

Wilderness First Aid Certification   2018

Entry-level medical training in wilderness medicine

Additional Skills & Interests

- **Proficient in:** Adobe Creative Suite, GarageBand, iMovie, and Microsoft Office
- **Languages:** French (fluent), Dutch (conversational)
- **Hiking:** Completed a self-planned expedition of Pacific Crest Trail and group treks through Alaska, Pyrenees Mountains, and Greater Wyoming Basin

STATEMENT/GOAL: A financial analyst with modeling expertise and the ability to inspire teamwork and lead peer groups.

SKILL SET #1: Earnest Worker	SKILL SET #2: Team Leader	SKILL SET #3: Creative Thinker & Explorer
EXAMPLES	**EXAMPLES**	**EXAMPLES**
1. Developed financial models for pitch stocks	**1.** Peer Academic Advisor	**1.** Pacific Crest Trail Guide
2. Prepared tax returns for S-corps, trusts, and individuals	**2.** Outstanding Delegate, Model UN Nations	**2.** Youngston English Department Scholarship
3. Detailed client portfolio analysis	**3.** Team Captain, Club Water Polo	**3.** Self-taught Dutch speaker
STORY	**STORY**	**STORY**
• **Premier Global**—Helped construct a financial model to compare pitch stocks across the real estate and energy sectors for a client's new investment product. I was able to deliver a comprehensive model a month ahead of schedule.	• **Model UN**—Named head of delegation my junior year. The competition proved to be especially challenging, and I was able to revitalize our team. We went from unrecognized on day one to finishing third overall by the end of the final day.	• **Wilderness Expedition**—Partnered with U.S. Forest Service to prepare, map, and accommodate for one of the most difficult outdoor expeditions in the U.S. Learned how to make adjustments to keep a team motivated and focused on a common goal.

Victoria's Messaging Document

When we met Victoria, we reviewed her resume and saw the expected experience for a competitive entry-level analyst role. But we also saw some hidden leadership skills through her extracurricular activities and a real curiosity and quest for adventure in her venture down the Pacific Crest Trail. We learned she was a real hiking enthusiast and has a "can-do" attitude about a lot of things. We wanted to be sure a potential employer saw those qualities as well.

In her messaging document, we landed on three themes: Earnest Worker, Team Leader, and Creative Thinker and Explorer. She may never say these three themes out loud, but we want her experiences lined up in these three categories, because it helps her align her responses to these examples and share specific stories that prove them. It focuses her on being able to share specific stories that map to her experiences in these three areas, because we believe these three themes will distinguish her from other candidates.

And as we roleplay an interview, we'll put the document in front of her and coach her to hear a question and line it up to one of the three themes before she responds. (More on answering questions in Chapter 25.)

Mid-Career: Duncan Dexter

Duncan is solid mid-career. He loves the gaming industry and thinks he's ready for a senior sales leadership role. From his perspective, Last Frontier is the leader in the industry and he's eager to return there and run the show. It will be highly competitive to win the senior sales role at this top gaming company. Review his resume, and you'll see that he's done most of the things you would expect to see on a sales leader's resume.

DUNCAN DEXTER

Seattle, WA
123-456-7890 • myemail@me.com
LinkedIn.com/in/Duncan-dexter

SALES AND RELATIONSHIP MANAGEMENT LEADER
A compassionate sales leader with the vision, experience, and skills needed to drive sales revenue and strengthen customer satisfaction during business disruption and accelerated growth.

CORE COMPETENCIES

Leading...	Collaborating...	Building...
Growth Strategies	Cross-Functional Teams	Strategic Partnerships
Team Retention & Development	Project & Program Management	Customer Relationships

PURPLE COW GAMING – Redmond, WA   2016–2021

$12 billion top gaming company providing console, digital, and experiential gaming to over 150 million players.

Senior Director – Channel Partners (2016–2017)

Recruited a team of fifteen channel managers to new organization for Channel Partnerships

- Created messaging, contracts, and promotional marketing to increase visibility
- Drove strategy to strengthen partner value, which improved negotiations and created exclusivity with top accounts
- Attracted forty-five new partners in program's first year
- Generated 70% of lead expectations and activity
- Delivered 110% of sales goal with partners

LAST FRONTIER GAMING (LF) – Redwood City, CA   2013–2016

Premier gaming company in the U.S and European markets, providing innovative gaming experiences to more than 300 million registered players.

Senior Director – Relationship Management (2013–2016)

Directed team of thirty+ field organizations (five managers; twenty-five individual contributors)

- Developed strategy to increase renewal results by 50%
- Built high-performing teams, measured by customer retention, revenue growth, and customer satisfaction
- Drove nine consecutive quarters of historic growth in subscription packages
- Led division through acquisition of three new gaming franchises within eighteen months

FINAL ADVENTURE GAMING – Mountain View, CA   2010–2013

A $1.5 billion provider of entertainment products, cherished franchises, and advanced software design with more than 150 million users.

Director, Relationship Management – National Accounts (2011–2013)

Led and mentored team that managed top thirty revenue-producing customers

- Delivered FY'13 revenues 109% over FY'10 to $53.2 million
- Renewed $12+ million in contracts, and $3 million in new product sales

Associate Director, Channel Sales Operations (2010–2011)

Led team that had responsibility for new product rollout to high-profile retailers

- Delivered FY'11 revenues 110% over previous year
- Renewed $8 million+ in contracts, and $30 million in new product sales (150% of annual goal)

AURASPHERE – San Mateo, CA   2006–2010

An industry-leading gaming design company, serving over 30 million users in 150 countries.

Senior Manager, Account Management (2008–2010)

Senior Manager, Sales Operations (2007–2008)

Manager – Special Projects and Business Development (2006–2007)

THE ANDERSON GROUP – Charleston, SC   2001 – 2006

Regional software distributor for project management platforms.

Manager, Business Development

Associate, Account Management

EDUCATION:

MBA – Kellogg School of Business, Northwestern University   2008

BA, Art History – University of Washington, St. Louis   2001

STATEMENT/GOAL: A compassionate sales leader with the vision, experience, and skills needed to drive sales revenue and strengthen customer satisfaction during business disruption and accelerated growth.

SKILL SET #1: Sales Leader	SKILL SET #2: Collaborative Partner	SKILL SET #3: Industry Expertise & Visibility
EXAMPLES	**EXAMPLES**	**EXAMPLES**
1. 50% increased renewal revenue in twelve months	**1.** Acquired three gaming brands within eighteen months	**1.** Conference keynotes **2.** Fifteen years of industry experience
2. New subscriptions campaign success	**2.** Consolidated vendors through Final Adventure acquisition of Aurasphere	**3.** Managed 300 partnerships with distributors
3. Team recruitment and development	**3.** Created Channel Partners organization	
STORY	**STORY**	**STORY**
• **Last Frontier**—Launched subscription package to new and existing consumers, driving historic company growth across three quarters. The success of the package drove a 50% increase in renewed revenue within twelve months as well as completing 140% of our anticipated revenue goals.	• **Vendor Consolidation**—Led the acquisition of three new franchise titles and administered the transition with buyers and retail distributors. During this time, our revenue win rate increased by 15% and our customer satisfaction score increased by nearly 20%.	• **Taking a Selfie**—My favorite part of my job is the part I play in bringing consumer's favorite genres to the marketplace. People I don't know come up and ask to take a picture with me...I've never forgotten how it makes me feel. I do it for the gamers!

Duncan's Messaging Document

When we met Duncan, we learned that he was narrowly focused on his dream job at the top gaming company. A recruiter called him because he was in the industry, but we weren't sure how seriously they were considering him. It can be tough to return to a company in a much more senior position! We tightened up the resume above to illustrate measurable outcomes. We wanted a recruiter or company leader to see that Duncan drives results. But as we heard more about the opportunity, we realized that the company had grown significantly through acquisitions and didn't seem to be slowing down. We knew he would be questioned about change management. Remember that from the talent-acquisition insights?

Duncan had been through many merger & acquisition steps, but they didn't come through on his resume. We focused his messaging document to be sure that he was positioned as a leader who could thrive in disruption. We rewrote his positioning statement and mapped out themes to help him talk about disruption as well as sales results.

His themes were *Sales Leader, Collaborative Partner,* and *Industry Expertise & Visibility.* We thought that to be an attractive candidate, he would need to illustrate his visibility within the industry and his ability to achieve results during the chaos of change. By organizing his experience into these three themes, he was able to think about what it takes to help an organization keep moving forward in terms of sales revenue, vendor and partner management, and industry opportunities and to talk about vision and direction. He had all of it, and when we packaged it he was able to position himself as someone who had the right toolkit, but also as the right kind of leader for a company that has more disruption ahead.

Peak Career: Bernard Haas

Bernard is a seasoned HR leader and, judging by his resume, he seems to be well-rounded in talent steps as well as benefits experience. He is heavily recruited across multiple industries because his work on company cultures has become known through industry events. In fact, he's publishing his "Own Your Culture" playbook next year.

He seems to fit the typical HR profile. And yet, if you scroll down his resume, you'll see he's actually a lawyer by training. And, as we soon learned, there's much more to his brand than his resume suggests.

Bernard Haas

777 Main Street

Beaverton, OR

LinkedIn.com/in/bernardhaas

C: (123) 456-7890

O: (198) 765-4321

myemail@me.com

EXECUTIVE MANAGEMENT – Human Resources

A veteran HR leader with the desire and experience to help companies execute "people priorities" while delivering employee satisfaction, great customer experiences, and business results.

CORE COMPETENCIES

- Corporate Responsibility
- Change Management
- Executive Leadership
- Culture Development
- Employee Lifecycle
- Compensation & Benefits

PROFESSIONAL EXPERIENCE

Pineapple Software – Portland, Oregon — 2016–Present

Chief People Officer

- Managed a global team of 100+ employees, with a combined budget of over $30M
- Developed and executed global strategy for talent acquisition and retention in five emerging markets
- Engaged top leaders with "People Priorities" culture playbook and lifted employee satisfaction by 30%
- Oversaw the global rollout of multi-tiered learning and development initiatives
- Led a North American strategy to strengthen talent metrics by 50% within six months
- Formulated, communicated, and implemented HR policy involving recruitment, placement, position management, pay administration, and employee relations across four organizations
- Successfully onboarded, trained, and developed 300 new employees in three years
- Launched inaugural six-month rotation program "New Manager Bootcamp"
- Launched inaugural twelve-month group coaching curriculum for VPs

NeoSpace – Boston, Massachusetts — 2014–2016

Senior VP – Culture & Talent

- Implemented a global program for evaluating performance and providing feedback
- Developed internal engagement strategies, including learning and development programs and online learning platforms
- Worked with leadership team to conceptualize a culture that illustrates values and people priorities
- Built campaign to strengthen culture and improved employee satisfaction by 40%
- Advised leaders across the company on all issues and risks related to employment in six different countries
- Managed communication and conversations to support a 20% talent reduction on technology teams
- Implemented a corporate university and wellness initiative for entire employee base

Red Rhino Automotive – Santa Monica, California — 2011–2014

Vice President, Human Resources

- Developed and advised leadership teams on HR and non-HR policies for compliance in fifteen countries
- Initiated leader compliance guidelines and training for harassment and discrimination policies
- Led the end-to-end execution of human capital strategy, including strategic planning, talent acquisition, employee experience, benefits and compensation, and performance reviews
- Redesigned corporate benefits package to allow for flexible work and part-time benefits
- Retained 90% of employees during ambitious business model transformation

Pacific Northwest Cruise Lines. – Los Angeles, California   2008–2011

Director – Talent Development

- Created a career-mapping process to manage a 40% growth in workforce over three years
- Worked in partnership with the executive team to develop and execute a talent strategy
- Designed an organization development project to support five-year strategic plan
- Oversaw a curriculum of fifty+ programs leveraging twenty external vendors to support 1000 employees

CDE Entertainment – Emeryville, California   2003–2008

HR Business Partner

Happy-Go-Lucky Toy Company – El Segundo, California   2000–2003

Senior Manager – Health Plans

Yurich, Bierman & Saunders, LLP – San Jose, California   1998–2000

Junior Attorney

Townson & Townson, LLP – Los Gatos, California   1996–1998

Junior Attorney

COMMUNITY INVOLVEMENT & INTERESTS

National Council of Chief People Officers – New York, New York   2020–2021

Board of Directors, Member

Portland Metro YMCA – Portland, Oregon

Board of Directors, President   2018–2019

Board of Directors, Chief Financial Officer   2016–2017

Holy Family School – Boston, Massachusetts   2014–2016

Board of Directors

ADDITIONAL HIGHLIGHTS

- Fluent in English, Spanish, German, and French
- Accomplished Industry Coach with two decades of experience championing industry trends and emerging talent
- Regional finalist for Westminster Dog Show, Terrier Group

Partner/Owner of Thistle Thorn (TT) Vineyard in Salem, Oregon

Certified Juris Doctor – University of San Francisco, School of Law, Certified Bar (*State of California*)

Executive MBA – *UCLA Anderson School of Management*

Political Science – UCLA

189

STATEMENT/GOAL: A veteran HR leader with the desire and experience to help companies execute "people priorities" while delivering employee satisfaction, great customer experiences, and business results.

SKILL SET #1: Servant Leader	SKILL SET #2: Teacher, Coach & Motivator	SKILL SET #3: Culture Junkie
EXAMPLES	EXAMPLES	EXAMPLES
1. Navigated employees' view through three business transformations	1. Global talent strategy that aligns commonalities and differences	1. Created a People Priorities playbook leveraged at three companies
2. Peer coaching on harassment and discrimination - from toxic to inclusive	2. Developed and launched more than fifteen comprehensive leadership programs	2. Built annual plan for reigniting culture feel at two companies – 30–40% lift in customer satisfaction and engagement
3. Overhauled benefits package for flexible and part-time workers	3. Designed Corporate University model with access to online and in-person formats	3. Industry-recognized coach
4. Strengthened talent metrics by 50%	4. Led and mentored more than forty high-potential cohorts	
STORY	STORY	STORY
• **YMCA Portland Board**— Led numerous fundraising campaigns for the Portland YMCA. Dedicated to giving back to the community and using fundraising skills to support a non-profit mission.	• **Law to Benefits**—Trained as a lawyer, but saw firsthand how difficult life can be for people without benefits. My parents were sole practitioners and I saw how stressful worries around health care and insurance could be. It led to a career change that brought me where I am today.	• **The Coaching Playbook**— Developed playbook for organizational coaching entitled Own Your Culture, Retain Your People. Combined decades of experience with how to shift a toxic culture to an award-winning, people-first environment.

Bernard's Messaging Document

When we met Bernard, we quickly learned that he wasn't just climbing a corporate ladder, even though he's done so quite well. Somewhere between his work on discrimination, harassment, and benefits he got a little burned out on process and realized that at the root of it he cares the most about people. He believes that culture makes all the difference in how people work, how people behave, and, ultimately, whether people feel empowered by their work and loyal to their companies. Bernard's vested in helping companies establish, maintain, and nurture "heart" within their organizations. While he's well-qualified to be a CHRO, he wants his next role to be more about people and less about HR process. His dream role is to work side by side with a founder on creating a culture that supports fast growth and human empowerment.

Through our discussion, we just kept uncovering the tapestry of Bernard's work and his career. His themes were *Servant Leader, Teacher, Coach, & Motivator*, and *Culture Junkie*. We knew that he wanted to move away from talking about HR benchmarks and spend more time evaluating companies' interest in culture and employee growth. And that's why his messaging document allows him to highlight his passion as much as his experience. He's already narrowed his interest by focusing on fast-growing, entrepreneurial companies. And his experience and interest will resonate with a founder who is equally vested in culture.

Recruiters and executive search teams don't like our messaging document. Many managers and leaders have told us that they share them with recruiters and have asked recruiters to share them along with their resumes. But recruiters don't want to do this, because it breaks with formality and makes those who use them stand out too much from other candidates. That's fair criticism. Messaging can't override a resume, but it can redirect a conversation.

We've also had people tell us that they have shared the document with an interviewer as a way of saying, "Here's what uniquely qualifies me for this role." And it seems to work. Every situation is different, and whether or not the document shows up in the interview is personal choice. But it's essential to prepare for the interview, and it's a great tool to organize the themes that highlight you in a memorable way.

24

Presence in an Interview

In Chapters 9 through 13, we talked in detail about personal style and impressions. But it's worth revisiting style to focus on what talent acquisition leaders have to say about impressions formed during an interview.

More than 95% of talent acquisition leaders say that candidates have to be able to listen to the questions being asked and answer them succinctly. They list the number one mistake as a lack of preparation. Candidates often seem unprepared and haven't researched the company or the role that they're interviewing for. This supports the old adage of "take an interest in us, and we will take an interest in you." Recruiters know that preparation impacts your confidence. They can tell quickly if you know what you're talking about and if you feel confident in your responses.

Here's what they say:

"Candidates should research companies, roles, and interviewers before the interview. You can tell very quickly if someone has given thought to their responses and matched their experience to a role."

- "You have to be able to connect with the interviewer, and the best way to do this is to provide examples of your accomplishments that seem relevant to our company and align with our values. And to do that, you need to know something about us."
- "Confidence shows up almost immediately and the lack of it reflects poorly on everything else we take in during an interview. While we may put forward a candidate who has some skill gaps, we never advance a candidate who lacks confidence."
- "Preparation is a big miss for peak-career leaders. They get interested in what's in it for them, and they skip right over research on culture, people, and the company."
- "You've got to be able to answer questions well. Start with the bottom line or headline and then add color or an example to your response. When you ramble, we rarely take note of what you've said."

We'll cover answering questions in Chapter 25.

Eye contact and expressiveness were the most important style elements that talent leaders called out. They're looking for candidates who seem passionate about the company and illustrate a level of conviction about the opportunity. Essentially, the recruiters validated our guidance on style attributes. Remember the Three C's: Confidence, Commitment, and Connection. Confidence shows up immediately and sets the stage for how interviewers listen to you. Commitment shows up in effort. Your expressiveness illustrates a little passion and desire to work for their company. And Connection, talking directly to the interviewers, is described as eye contact but manifests more as your ability to draw their interest and responses to your ideas.

Their specific thoughts:

- "We assess everything about you, from what you wear to how you enter the room and settle into the space."
- "When you meet someone who seems to have little awareness of body language and eye contact, you assume they are inexperienced. In fact, you weight the impact of their examples and stories based on how they come across as they share them."
- "Professionalism is still a defining characteristic. It's how you interact with staff and how you choose to put yourself together in appearance and attire for the interview."
- "Candidates miss with us in matching our passion and energy. If you don't match it, we're not interested."
- "The interview starts when you enter the building. At times, how you interact with security, assistants, or others in the building is all a part of the evaluation."
- "You should be as aware of your body language as the interviewer will be. This is an opportunity to position yourself. And everything about you is a part of that positioning."

Most interviews start in a virtual setting and, at the writing of this book, some candidates go through the entire hiring process virtually. Recruiters say that virtual impressions are harder. The natural flow of conversation and connection feels more stilted. They don't find it easy to read candidates over video, and most candidates don't show up as well over a virtual platform.

When candidates show up too casually and haven't given thought to the setting or the technology involved in participating in a virtual interview, recruiters think they don't take the interview seriously.

Unless you understand the virtual setting, it can be a disadvantage. The style attributes still apply, but the execution of choices with body, voice, and connection shifts a bit.

Let's revisit the three broad attributes and consider the virtual setting.

Confidence

In the virtual setting, confidence extends beyond how we see you and how you use your body. It becomes about everything we see when we adjust to a close-up view of a communicator and their setting. In an office setting, an interviewee never had responsibility for the setting. They went into an office, and the interviewer controlled the setting. But when a candidate turns on a laptop camera, they're inviting an interviewer into their setting and everything about that backdrop becomes a reflection of the candidate. It takes intention to find a quiet and uncluttered space for a good interview. It requires an understanding of the technology and good positioning of yourself in the camera view.

You should be positioned in the center of the screen with the camera view hitting you about mid-chest. When the shot is too close-up on your face, an interviewer notices a shift in your focus quickly. Adjust the camera view to allow the recruiter to see a little more of you. Make sure the camera hits you at eye level or a little higher. Never choose a view that looks up at you, as it distorts your size and makes eye contact seem as if you're looking down on the interviewer. In fact, you are.

Consider your lighting as well. Fluorescent lighting keeps offices bright. At home, you're more impacted by windows, sunlight, and shadows. An interviewer needs to be able to see your face without shadows. A brighter setting makes you seem more energetic, focused, and involved in a conversation. Light should be in front of you and behind your screen to improve brightness.

Commitment

The voice conveys a sense of energy and effort. In person, an interviewer would take in your voice pace and tone as a part of the total impression of how they see you and how they hear you. In a virtual setting though, recruiters say that the sound of the voice becomes significantly more important. And that's because, like all listeners, the recruiter may not stay focused on the view of you if video isn't being used or if your video is poor quality. This puts more pressure on voice quality and requires the interviewee to think about getting behind each thought and delivering ideas with a measured cadence.

You should practice talking through the concepts on your messaging document. Record your voice through a virtual platform or on your phone. Listen to responses and evaluate the pace and impact of your voice. You'll notice that it makes a difference in whether or not your key points are heard.

Connection

In a virtual setting, connection remains the concept of talking to someone and working for a response or reaction to your ideas. The camera becomes the interviewer and trying to read reactions gets clunkier. You talk to the interviewer through the camera, but you view their response in a virtual square. Interviewers say the eye contact, or lack of it, is the toughest part of a virtual interview. And this is because many interviewees don't seem to know where the camera is or how to talk directly through it. They seem to look down and all around. In the close-up shot, the lack of connection becomes obvious and distracting.

It takes practice to narrow your focus and talk to a camera. Practice this in a videotaped mock interview so that you can see how easy or challenging working with the camera is for you. It makes a difference in establishing impressions of honesty, sincerity, and warmth, so it's worth taking the time to learn how to do it well.

25

Interviews by Panel

We were also interested in the recruiters' perspectives on what's changed about interviewing. If you haven't been in the market in the last four to five years, you may be surprised by some of the trends that have taken hold.

The panel interview is one of those. While the more complex group interview used to be reserved for peak-career positions, it's now used for most positions. It's seen as more efficient for the company, and it's harder for the interviewee. Recruiters actually argue that it isn't as efficient as companies think, because it burdens and often stalls the process when additional interviewers are added in. The recruiters' challenge is managing people who join the process late and have to buy in to the role description, candidate qualifications, and the priorities set for selection. The more people involved, the harder it is for recruiters to help a group reach common shared objectives for the interview process.

In fact, recruiters say that interviewers can get too focused on personal interests and commonalities. Those conversations are easy for an interviewer to lead. They get to know the person but miss the evaluation of a skill set. You play tennis and I play tennis, so I like you. You're from Europe and I'm from Europe, so I trust you. Commonalities lead to comfort on both sides of an interview, and while recruiters know commonalities alone are a poor reason to hire someone, you can leverage them to your advantage as the interviewee.

Research on a company and interviewers will help you uncover commonalities. And when you find them, call them out. It helps with the light conversation before the details of the interview. It can also help you warm up a setting in follow-up interviews if you can remind an interviewer of the common ground and connection from a previous interview.

Whether or not the panel is efficient, it serves an important purpose on the interviewing side. It ensures that multiple stakeholders hear the same information and are working from the same experience to discuss impressions. As the interviewee, your goal is still to weave your three key themes throughout the interview. It's harder because you have to engage a room full of people in the process. The messaging document becomes an essential tool to help you do that.

Overall, it will be a more effective conversation if you can bridge ideas together and avoid interviewers who drive their own agendas and their own sets of questions. When this happens in a group of people, it can feel disjointed to you and to everyone who is listening to your responses.

Let's take Duncan from our mid-career interview as an example. His message themes were *Sales Leader, Collaborative Partner,* and *Industry Expertise & Visibility.* He's sitting in a panel interview with four leaders, two of whom seem to be driving the discussion: the CMO and the COO. The marketing leader picked up on the industry visibility theme as Duncan talked about his industry exposure and keynote events. The CMO likes Duncan's experience and willingness to deliver keynotes, and he keeps returning to the industry theme and asking more about trends and new ideas for leverage in their industry. The operations lead is more focused on sales growth and pushes for more detail on revenue growth and strategies. Duncan feels like he's in a ping-pong match: from trends to growth, from big-thinking possibilities to granular steps of sales rigor. It just isn't flowing well. He needs to bridge the ideas together like this:

"This is a great conversation, considering what's happening outside the company in your industry and what's happening inside the company each day to drive sales tactics. And while it's two very different perspectives, it might be helpful to bring them together and explain why I see both components as key elements of an overall sales playbook."

Ultimately, Duncan wants to keep most of the discussion connected so that he can drive home his central themes and not get pulled into tangents with different players. It takes practice, but the goal is to bridge from one interviewer to the next. Sometimes, the interviewers will help you do this; sometimes they don't. To help bridge the gap, you can always refer back to questions that were asked by a previous colleague.

"That's a great question, and it's similar to the point Patricia made earlier when she asked me about scaling an organization and onboarding quickly. I shared my experience in structuring a sales process, and your question connects the product integration team into that process. Let me talk more about the relationship between sales and integration and I'll tie it back to the overall sales process...."

As part of your preparation for a panel, research the interviewers in the room. Know what they do and how long they've done it. Consider their perspectives and priorities in running their function areas. When we help an interviewee prepare for the panel interview, we whiteboard the room and put the key players around a table. We talk through relationships and how different (and sometimes conflicting) perspectives may show up. This helps a candidate visualize the upcoming experience and begin to attach roles and perspectives to people.

And our talent leaders agreed. They say the ability to read the room is an important skill in a panel interview. You need to have awareness of how multiple people are reacting, and you need to be prepared to draw all of them into the conversation.

Having more players in a conversation can make it more dynamic or more disjointed. The interviewee can influence the outcome by managing questions well. There are two techniques that can improve an interviewee's ability to handle questions: adjusting the question and simplifying the answer.

Adjust the Question:

Believe it or not, most people hear a question and jump in to answer it without considering the question itself. That's how responses get misinterpreted and interviewees get caught over their skis. If you were in an interview and your resume mentioned global experience, you might get a question like this:

"So, Charlie, you seem to have a lot of global experience and that's interesting to us, as we expand into APAC next year. How would you build out a geographic team in APAC?"

Many Charlies will jump in and tell you how to build an international team...even though they haven't worked in APAC (Asia-Pacific). This interviewer is focused on APAC, so the next question will be... "Well, that's interesting, because most of our research is telling us that we shouldn't have an APAC strategy; we should have individual country strategies instead." Now Charlie is over his skis. He either has to backtrack and say he doesn't know the APAC market, or he'll continue with his position and dig a bigger hole.

Here's what he should have done to adjust the question to his "sweet spot" or base of knowledge.

When he's asked: "So Charlie, you seem to have a lot of global experience and that's interesting to us as we expand into APAC next year. How would you build out a geographic team in APAC?"

Charlie adjusts the question like this:

"My global experience was in Western Europe and it may not be a perfect match to the APAC market. Let me share with you how we set up our geographic team in Europe and we can compare it to your preliminary plans in APAC." With this lead-in to his response, Charlie doesn't minimize his international experience, but he clarifies where it was so he doesn't end up over his skis.

Every interviewee worries about unpredictable nature of questions. They fear that they won't have an answer for a strategy question or that they won't understand the level of detail being asked from a technical question. The miss is in trying to answer anything and everything.

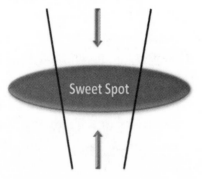

The visual above represents an interviewee's sweet spot, and we use this as a coaching tool to illustrate how to lower a question or lift one. When a question is broader than your expertise or the topic being discussed, you lower the question before answering it. Reframe the question in terms of what you do know, as Charlie did above. When a question is too specific, you adjust the question to pull it *up* to your sweet spot.

Charlie might be asked:

"In our CRM tool, we track IB calls, we track customer RPMS, and we track a sales rep's DAL. How do you leverage those metrics?" Charlie has no idea what they're pulling from their CRM, so he'll lift the altitude of the question.

"I'm not familiar with those acronyms and may not know your CRM system. But tell me more about what you're trying to track, and I can speak to sales activity as an early indicator of results." In both examples, the adjustment to the question keeps Charlie in his sweet spot and helps him stay confident about his ability to answer well.

Simplify the Answer:

The second skill is the ability to answer questions well. Questions are one of the least disciplined forms of communication and yet they should be the most structured. They can be an easy back-and-forth discussion. But when they're answered poorly, they signal to the interviewer that an interviewee is unfocused and unsure.

Most people get a question and begin talking their way to the answer.

Consider Cody, who was interviewing for a director role to lead a platform integration team. The interviewer was intrigued with Cody's experience in aligning multiple teams in a customer's organization to a new solution. So the interviewer asked, "Cody, how long does a typical platform integration take?"

And Cody started talking.

"That's a great question because there are a lot of factors to consider. There are probably at least four customer teams in an integration like this and you have to figure out how updated their software is before you start. They're all different. Some are up to date; others are behind. Then, you have to look at their priorities and your time for the install and that varies significantly based on time of year and the departments involved. So, it gets complicated."

What's the answer? There really wasn't one. If you're the interviewer, you realize Cody didn't get to the answer. You make a note of it and, if it continues to happen, Cody's not your guy.

The better way to answer a question is to follow a three-step process.

1. **Give a one-sentence answer.** Be direct in answering the questions right up front. The first part of your answer will get the most attention from the leader.
2. **Expand the concept.** Provide two to three additional sentences to support the one-sentence answer.
3. **Provide an example.** Share an example to illustrate your point.

A good answer has structure to it, which makes it easy to follow. The model suggests that, rather than talking your way to a definitive answer, you should start with a definitive response and then expand on it. It helps a listener hear a definitive answer to their question and supports the impression that you are someone who is clear and confident.

Cody knew the answer; he just didn't structure it well. Here's what changes about his response.

"Cody, how long does a typical platform integration take?"

"Typically, an integration takes three to six months." **(One-sentence answer)**

"That's a pretty significant range, and let me explain why. There are usually four customer teams in an integration, and you need to know how updated their software is before you start. Some will be up to date; others will be behind. It also depends on priorities of each department and the time of year of the install." **(Expand the concept)**

"Interestingly, the most complicated integration I've led only took three months because the customer departments prioritized it. And our slowest one was six months because the department hadn't updated their software and we had to run through updates before the integration began." **(Example)**

The flow of the response provides an easy way for the interviewer to follow the response. And it creates two opportunities (the expanded concept and the example) for the interviewer to jump in and continue the back-and-forth discussion.

In a panel interview, the ability to deliver clear responses and connect those responses for everyone in the room is a differentiator. Learning to answer questions well is a skill that you'll leverage not only in interviews but in any leadership role. It's a discipline that defines a communicator as clear and articulate, and it sets up our final theme, which suggests that you should think beyond the interview to how you position yourself consistently across your career.

Section IV

Building Your Career Narrative

26

Your Career Story

With disruption becoming more and more frequent in our lives, you'll need to be able to position yourself beyond the structure of a formal interview. You'll need to be able to give an elevator pitch of your experiences, a summary of your accomplishments, and an overview of who you are as a person and the beliefs and values that drive you. And in order to be successful at all of that, you'll need to be able to do what so many people dread: talk about yourself.

No one likes to do this. When someone asks us the infamous question, "So tell me about yourself," most people struggle to think of what to say. Even when we're expecting the question, something about being put on the spot and asked to simplify something as complex as our life story into a few sentences feels too daunting. Even in informal conversations, most people will grab on to something factual and start to recite their history like they're reading something they might've submitted for a job posting.

"Well, I went to the University of Cincinnati…" "I worked for P&G for a number of years…" "I just moved to Seattle last May…"

Remember what we discussed about the importance of commitment and speaking with conviction. If you're the listener and you hear someone begin to list off facts that you already knew, how interested are you in continuing this conversation? Not very, right? And yet as the communicator, you were asked to talk about the one thing you know the most about: yourself! How can you be disconnected from a listener when the topic is one you know so well?

One of the biggest reasons is that many people don't consider their career paths to be an incredible journey. Most feel as though their career is a mix of happenstance, right-place-at-the-right-time, and adjusting to changes in their lives outside of work. It wouldn't fill a best-selling novel, so we assume it's not worth telling.

But that isn't so. Everyone has a few compelling stories within them, and it's the telling of these stories that lets you share *you*. They're what makes you unique and interesting to a listener. Talking about yourself helps people get to know you and trust you. Your stories make you real. They also make you vulnerable.

And that's another reason people don't like to talk about themselves. Career journeys aren't just limited to successes. In fact, most journeys have more challenges than successes. They're crooked paths with dead ends, roadblocks, and even a few falls. And many people worry that sharing more about where you're from, what you've tried, and where you've failed will somehow fall short of a listener's expectations. But that's what listeners crave in settings from interviews to center-stage keynotes. They want a way to relate to you and see a glimpse of what you might have in common.

Yet this is where most people struggle, and it's because they just don't know how to tell their own stories well.

Case in point:

A few years ago, we attended a meet and greet where a famous founder and entrepreneur was being interviewed as part of the main event. He drew a large crowd, and our team was excited to see what he had to say.

The speaker talked about his accomplishments. He told the audience about selling his first company, meeting his wife, and selling his second company, and about the various mental exercises he had performed, from taking an ice shower every morning to running a hundred miles.

On paper, that sounds like prime material for an entertaining story! But ten minutes into the interview, the thrill and excitement seemed to vanish from the room. Many people had snapped pictures when he started, but after only a few minutes they were checking emails, with only a few diligent front-rowers still paying attention. The storyteller shared great experiences. He had a big smile and an open, relaxed confidence. But the audience quickly lost interest in what he was saying.

For an hour, he went through the steps of building successful businesses and the highlights of experiences he'd had with celebrities in remote locations. But not once did he relate anything he said to the people sitting in the room listening to him. His stories came across as a canned speech, and he seemed to the audience like a distant celebrity half-heartedly reading his own biography.

Here's where he missed the mark:

Storytelling is not about you, it's about making a connection with your listener. And for the most part, people are interested in your *journey*, not your triumphs. This is the core element of storytelling. Connection with a listener isn't about great outcomes or successes. It's about the challenge or the unexpected curve.

As interesting as it might seem at first to hear a story about someone taking a polar bear plunge into a frozen lake with an ex-Marine as the first part of his self-created mental health retreat, the speaker in the example above did nothing to connect that experience to his audience. The room was filled with hard-working professionals, none of whom owned a private jet or could relate to the luxury of creating their own military-inspired training program.

But I'd be willing to bet they could've related to a story about misalignment, or a story about what it was like to be starting out after college with no money, away from family and friends, with no idea what they were meant to do with their life. In that speaker's rich history of successes, there must have been at least a few stories of triumph over adversity, feelings of hopelessness just before a saving grace, or experiencing utter exhaustion and defeatedly thinking, "There's just no way this will ever work."

Those are the kind of stories we attach to and they're the ones that we remember and repeat.

- Henry Ford developed the assembly line…and launched an industrial revolution.

- Grace Hopper created the first universal programming language...and catapulted the capabilities of computers forward.
- Ann Tsukamoto discovered how to isolate human stem cells...and saved hundreds of thousands of lives.
- Steve Jobs started tinkering in a garage...and revolutionized the way we connect with each other.

This is the core element of storytelling. Connecting with a listener does not come from great outcomes and successes, but through overcoming challenges and unexpected curves. And that's what makes it hard to talk about ourselves. Most of us think about storytelling as an example of "How I Built This" or "How I Accomplished This." But storytelling is how we humanize ourselves to our listeners and how we show our strengths through hard-fought battles and experiences earned.

It's a hard thing to map out, because you lived it and you don't always see it. It's less a chronology of everything you've done and more the cumulative learnings that shape who you've become and the stories you use to bring those learnings to life.

Over the years we've helped countless managers and leaders tell their stories through our three-step process: **Map the Journey, Define Your Experiences,** and **Bring It to Life!**

Map the Journey

When we work with someone to build out their career narrative, the first thing we want to know is what they've done and where they've been. We start from the early days of their life and track every step leading to their current role. It's a free-flowing content fountain where we want to capture as much of the picture as we can. Sometimes we do this on a map; sometimes we do this on a timeline. This helps us see the highlights and low points of someone's journey in perspective. From there, we can build the full picture of that person and identify the top themes that make their experiences truly unique.

Define Your Experiences

Within a person's experiences, there are always some personal traits that seem to matter the most to them. It's never the same between two people. But there are often patterns that help you think about the key themes of who you are that you'd want to describe to someone. We call those your key learnings, and we often identify them as the traits of your leadership. These are the specific themes you can use to build out your career narrative and tie your personal experiences to your professional expertise.

Bring It to Life

And lastly, every journey has stories. But many communicators make the mistake of trying to tell too many stories or trying to tell a story without purpose. The last step of building your career journey is to identify three or four stories that will intrigue a listener and support the themes you want the listener to remember about you. And once you've settled on those stories, you need to learn to tell them really well!

When your career story is complete, it's no longer the unstructured response to the vague question, "So, tell me about yourself…" It's your story told in a manner that adds interest and meaning for listeners. It has highs and lows that engage a group and make you seem more "normal" than they might have assumed. And that's pretty inspiring to any group.

In the following chapters we'll revisit Victoria, Duncan, and Bernard and show you how we would help each of them build out their career journey. And within their journeys, we hope you can find the inspiration and road map to begin to build out your own!

27

Step One: Map Your Journey

If you've ever written a term paper, a legal brief, a novel, or anything in between, you've probably heard the mantra that it's easier to have too much content and edit it down rather than trying to stretch too little content. And the same is true with your career narrative.

When we work with someone to build out their narrative, the first thing we do is ask them to tell us their life story. No small task! But without referencing their resume or thinking through their career specifics, we want them just to talk to us about their family, where they grew up, their likes and dislikes…the list goes on and on. We love these conversations, and while we listen to someone talk we're busy filling out one of our 30 ft. by 8 ft. whiteboards. By the time we're done, there's rarely any white space left!

Here's why we do this:

While no one knows you better than *you*, it can often be hard to see your own defining characteristics amidst all the experiences you've had in your life. Forcing someone to go through the exercise of describing their background helps us draw out the person behind the facts. Remember that what a listener is really looking for in an interview or any social or professional setting is a form of connection or common ground with you. And once you have a clear portrait of yourself laid out across a whiteboard or a dining room table, it becomes much easier to identify those unique characteristics that you want to showcase to a listener.

When we go through this exercise as coaches, it helps us pinpoint what we as listeners found interesting, which in turn helps guide questions to explore an experience in more detail:

- "You've been to fifteen different countries in three years...why the desire to travel so much?"
- "You're a devoted Kiss fan...how did that happen?"
- "You've volunteered with the Red Cross for nearly a decade...why the special connection?"
- "You're a regional Sudoku champion...what other kinds of puzzles do you like to solve?"

These are the kind of personal touches that may not show up or come across on a resume, but that guide your decision-making process and show a listener much more about who you really are. And with a little structure, they can help you position your upbringing, personal interests, and hobbies as tangible and interesting professional experiences.

- An avid traveler...becomes a candidate with global experience.
- A devoted Kiss fan...becomes a candidate with a passion for unique cultures.

- A Red Cross volunteer...becomes a candidate who is devoted to helping others.
- A Sudoku champion...becomes a candidate who love to solve complex problems.

When you map out your own journey, you begin to see these unique characteristics fall into place. And once they do, they become the six or seven themes you'll use to frame how you want to position yourself to a listener.

To see how this process unfolds, let's take a look at our three fictional professionals again. When Victoria, Duncan, and Bernard completed the Map Your Journey exercises, here's what we learned about them:

Victoria (Early Career)

Victoria is the youngest of six kids. Both her parents are engineers, and her father works for a large oil and gas company. Her family lived in The Hague, the Netherlands for three years, following her father's job, and she attended eighth through tenth grade two blocks away from the United Nations building. She is fluent in French and can get by conversationally in Dutch.

Growing up, all five of Victoria's older siblings played soccer. She still remembers telling her parents that she didn't care what sport she played, so long as it wasn't soccer! She found a water polo club team at school and leapt at the chance to play because it was the one sport whose practice time fit within her parents' crazy carpool schedule.

It was also during this time that she discovered drama class and quickly fell in love with all things related to stagecraft.

Back in the U.S. she starred as Belle in her school's production of *Beauty and the Beast* and quickly gravitated to improv comedy at Northern Illinois.

In her free time, Victoria's favorite thing to do is to curl up by the window (especially in the rain!) with a good book. Spy novels are her favorite and she has read twenty of them this past year. She hopes to write and publish her own series one day.

Victoria and her family are all big hikers. Her parents hiked the Appalachian Trail together before they started a family, and to this day every family vacation has always had at least one or two major hikes baked into the itinerary.

As a listener, how are you feeling about Victoria now? Does she seem more "real" to you than she did from just her resume? Hopefully the answer is yes! In an early career setting, you're able to include much more of yourself in your actual resume. You don't have as many experiences to edit what gets covered. But even so, without this exercise, you wouldn't have known that Victoria was one of six children, or that she lived in the Netherlands, or that she was an aspiring spy novelist.

That's what this exercise is designed to do; pull out the experiences and events that make you who you are. And as we begin to pull together Victoria's narrative, these are the touchpoints that we'll draw from.

Duncan (Mid-Career)

Duncan was born and raised in Charleston, South Carolina. He was adopted, although people tell him all the time that he looks like his parents' biological child. Growing up, his uncle owned a shrimping boat and Duncan spent every weekend and summer before college helping his uncle haul in tons and tons of Atlantic shrimp. As a result, Duncan can't eat seafood without remembering the overpowering fishy smell that always seemed to drape over him like a blanket.

Unfortunately Duncan lost both of his parents in a car crash in 2006. Devastated, he moved out West for a fresh start and went to live in his college buddy's garage apartment. Shortly afterward, he found himself working at a video game console company, Aurasphere, where he admitted to his recruiter that he'd never played a video game before.

He worked through the acquisition of Aurasphere by Final Adventure Gaming, and, by chance, found himself working on a pirate-themed franchise game. Duncan hadn't stepped on a boat since he left Charleston four years before, and he described to us how this project was what rekindled his love of sailing. Reinspired, he joined a local sailing club and met his husband at the very first meeting!

Duncan is a self-described candy addict, specifically unique and exotic types of candy. He has a particular affinity for a type of sourball from Sri Lanka that he orders bulk shipments of every other month. Currently, Duncan is working on a side project with a friend to create a small "Candy of the Month" subscription club to showcase his favorites and introduce consumers to candies from around the world.

As a listener, how do you feel about Duncan? Duncan's story has some very unhappy moments, but also some unexpected twists and turns that have made him who he is. As you read about him, you're probably forming a picture of what he looks like in your mind. Maybe you have an idea of what his Charleston accent sounds like or maybe you could smell the shrimp odor hanging around him for days at a time. Those are the elements of storytelling, and we'll come back to those in Chapter 29.

But regardless of how you're picturing Duncan, you're viewing a much more complete person (perhaps even a very different person) than the picture you formed when you looked at the resume of a career salesperson. And that's what we're looking for in this exercise: the real you behind the statistics.

Bernard (Peak Career)

Bernard is Swiss-American. His parents immigrated to the United States in 1965 and set up their careers as lawyers in San Jose, California. Bernard was raised Catholic and he still attends mass every Sunday. His older sister has taught German at San Jose State for decades and Bernard himself is fluent in English, Spanish, German, and French.

In college, Bernard studied abroad in Chile for a year. There he developed a passion for South American artwork and now has a sizable collection of paintings, sculptures, and masks. He's an amateur collector and is always on the hunt for his next great addition.

Bernard met his wife, Isabella, in law school at the University of San Francisco. She has remained a corporate counsel throughout her career, but Bernard made a unique career switch in 2000. His parents were sole practitioners throughout their law careers, and while they were skilled at their work, Bernard remembers his father's constant worry and stress about health care and insurance claims. That stayed with Bernard all throughout law school, and after four years of practicing law, Bernard finally realized that what he was most passionate about was making sure people had good benefits behind their careers. That's when he made the switch to a benefits HR role and never looked back.

During a scuba diving expedition with his son, Bernard suffered an accident and severely damaged his right eardrum. As a result, he is now partially deaf, although he is quite good-humored about it and says he'd been searching his whole life for an excuse to not have to drive anymore.

Bernard is an avid wine enthusiast and is a part owner of a new vineyard in Oregon. In addition, both he and his wife are dog lovers and frequently describe themselves as parents to three children (two human and one canine). It's a point of personal pride for Bernard that his Airedale terrier, Major, made it into the preliminary Westminster Dog Show Trials back in 2012.

Bernard has chaired numerous Boards during his career, but the one he's most proud of is his affiliation with the Portland Metro YMCA. People have routinely told Bernard that he is *very* good at raising money, something that Bernard himself finds embarrassing, but, he admits, seems to be true. Bernard's favorite pastime is playing Chinese Checkers with his daughter, who, despite repeated attempts, "Hasn't beat the old man yet!"

As a listener, what do you think about Bernard? He's something of a man of the world, isn't he? From his resume, you might gather that Bernard was experienced in his field and had a variety of past experiences. But would you have imaged he was a South American art collector? Or a scuba diver? Or that he'd entered a world-renowned show dog contest?

From these three examples, you can see how different the person behind the resume might be from who you first imagined. And while all three of these professionals have had compelling experiences, it's not enough just to have had them. You have to know which experiences to pull from and how to frame them for a listener. And now that we've mapped out each of their journeys, we're ready to take the next step and define the experiences within their narratives.

28

Step Two: Define Your Experiences

In Chapter 23, we introduced you to the concept of the messaging document that we use to help someone think through how to frame their top themes ahead of an interview. But now we need to go back and explore how to select the attributes you want to weave into your career story.

Regardless of the setting you're preparing your career narrative for, you should have between six to seven key themes that you believe represent you. Depending on the setting where you're sharing these themes, you may choose to highlight certain themes over others, but you should always aim to have a solid half-dozen you can pull from when needed. And to find the right themes, this is where the exercise shifts from mapping the entirety of your experiences and interests to looking for patterns within your experiences that can support the traits you want to be known for.

Once you've fully mapped out your journey, you have your full repertoire of experiences to draw on to help build your leadership brand. So, what characteristics should you be looking for within your journey?

This is a great time to refer back to your personal brand map from Chapter 6. How would you describe your brand? What are the attributes that you think best describe who you are and what are the attributes you value most in yourself? In this part of building your narrative, you're looking for literal experiences across your career journey to support the key characteristics of your brand. We call this "finding the color."

For example, let's say you believe a key attribute of your brand is that you're a highly organized person. Well, why are you an organized person? What examples can you draw on from your experiences (either personal or professional) to convey to a listener that being an organized person is a key pillar of who you are as an employee or a leader?

Maybe you worked in a research lab where *everything* was color-coded and alphabetically and categorically sorted, and that level of organization has stayed with you ever since. Maybe your mother held competitions between you and your sister to see who could keep their room the cleanest and every week the winner got an extra dollar in their allowance. Or maybe you were once late to an important job interview because your kitchen was so cluttered you couldn't find your car keys and you vowed never to be that disorganized again.

These are the sort of examples that add color to your career narrative and give you a degree of credibility with a listener. Most won't just take your word that you're an organized person – you have to be able to illustrate it. These examples will also lead to compelling stories about yourself. But for this step, focus on identifying your top traits and look for examples of when a certain theme shone through or why it exists.

Let's go back to our three professionals and see how their experiences draw out their key characteristics.

Victoria (Early Career)

In the last chapter, we learned a *lot* more about Victoria. We learned that she lived in Amsterdam for three years, that she's one of six siblings, and that she's a superfan of spy novels. Now we need to frame up some of that color within her career-mapping and pull out some key characteristics she could draw on. She might connect examples like this:

- *Team Leader*: She's been a part of theater productions and an improv troupe.
- *Proven Captain*: She's held leadership positions from Water Polo Captain to head of her college's Model UN team.
- *Creative Explorer*: She's planned long-term hiking expeditions and has dabbled in novel-writing.
- *Family-Oriented*: She's a part of a big family that takes hiking vacations together every year.
- *Earnest Worker*: She kept working on that difficult algorithm for a client until she figured it out.
- *Global Traveler*: She's lived and studied abroad and speaks three languages.

Some of these examples you'll recognize from Victoria's first messaging document, but some are new. And it will be up to Victoria to decide which examples make sense to talk about depending on her audience. If she's interviewing for an analyst role within a company, she might choose to present herself as an *Earnest Worker, Proven Captain,* and *Creative Explorer.* Or if she's introducing herself to a peer cohort, she might focus on *Family-Oriented, Global Traveler* and *Team Leader.* The leading traits might shift, but both are authentic snapshots of the same career journey. See Victoria's expanded messaging document below:

MESSAGING DOCUMENT: VICTORIA PFLUGER

STATEMENT/GOAL: A financial analyst with modeling expertise and the ability to inspire teamwork and lead peer groups.

SKILL SET #1: Earnest Worker	SKILL SET #2: Team Leader	SKILL SET #3: Creative Thinker & Explorer
EXAMPLES	**EXAMPLES**	**EXAMPLES**
1. Developed financial models for pitch stocks	1. Peer Academic Advisor	1. Pacific Crest Trail Guide
2. Prepared tax returns for S-corps, trusts and individuals	2. Outstanding Delegate, Model UN Nations	2. Youngston English Department Scholarship
3. Detailed client portfolio analysis	3. Team Captain, Club Water Polo	3. Self-taught Dutch speaker
STORY	**STORY**	**STORY**
• **Premier Global**—Helped construct a financial model to compare pitch stocks across the real estate and energy sectors for a client's new investment product. I was able to deliver a comprehensive model a month ahead of schedule.	• **Model UN**—Competition was especially challenging, and I was able to revitalize our team. We went from unrecognized on day one to finishing third overall by the end of the final day.	• **Wilderness Expedition**—Partnered with U.S. Forest Service to prepare, map, and accommodate for one of the most difficult outdoor expeditions in the U.S. Learned how to make adjustments to keep a team motivated and focused on a common goal.
• **Wilson, Lalter & Solomon**—Developed proficiency with XYZ tax software while assisting with customer records and returns.	• **Water Polo Championship**—Guided my team to a regional championship while working through difficult team dynamics. Split captain vote between me and a senior. Was able to overcome and lead team to victory.	• **Novel-Writing**—Captivated by spy novels from James Bond to Jason Bourne. Have completed half of my first novel.
• **Peer Advisor**—Maintained high grade point average to be appointed Academic Peer Advisor. Assisted fellow students with core classes including Variable Calculus & Microeconomics.	• **Laughing Guild**—First freshman elected President of the improv troupe. Managed booking calendar for weekly events, club fundraisers, and comedic tournaments.	• **Studied Abroad**—Have taken classes in English and French and have visited twenty countries over the span of five years.

No matter the themes you identify in your own career narrative, the important thing is to be able to back them up with examples and learn how to share the parts of yourself that you think will best connect with your listener. Having an established and practiced road map will allow you to pivot your messaging as needed.

Duncan (Mid-Career)

Duncan's mapping exercise brought out some more vulnerable pieces. We learned that he's adopted and that he lost both his parents shortly after graduating college. We learned how he met his husband and that he has an insatiable sweet tooth. Just like we did with Victoria, now we need to take Duncan's experiences and pull out the best characteristics for him to build his narrative around. He might consider:

- *Compassionate Leader*: He knows what it's like to feel alone or upset and so he makes it a point to take care of his people.
- *Collaborative Partner*: He's cut his chops through a difficult corporate merger and moved himself cross-country.
- *Candy Entrepreneur*: He's starting his own "Candy of the Month" subscription service.
- *Consumer Advocate*: He loves the passion people feel for the products he sells. It's what fuels him!
- *Convivial Colleague*: He's an outgoing guy, and he tries to make every sailing outing as fun for his crewmates as his uncle made his for him on his shrimp boat.
- *Skilled Salesman:* …and he's got the numbers to prove it!

Just like with Victoria, you can recognize some of the themes we chose for Duncan's messaging document, but you also see some new ones, some of which will require Duncan to be a little vulnerable in order to share that part of his story. Your stories are your own, and you should never feel pressure to share a piece of yourself that you don't feel comfortable sharing yet. But as communication coaches, we would tell you that the more you can weave who you are into your overarching career narrative, the more connection you'll make with your listeners.

Imagine how much more compelling Duncan's positioning as a compassionate sales leader would be if he was able to share some of his own experiences. He might be able to quell a team's anxiety or convince a recruiter that his first priority as a manager is to take care of his people, because he knows the value of having someone who is there for you. Rather than just saying he cares about his people, Duncan can give a listener a firsthand account of why it matters to him that people feel supported.

Here's his expanded messaging document:

STATEMENT/GOAL: A compassionate sales leader with the vision, experience, and skills needed to drive sales revenue and strengthen customer satisfaction during business disruption and accelerated growth.

SKILL SET #1: Sales Leader	SKILL SET #2: Collaborative Partner	SKILL SET #3: Industry Expertise & Visibility
EXAMPLES	**EXAMPLES**	**EXAMPLES**
1. 50% increased renewal revenue in twelve months	1. Acquired three gaming brands within eighteen months	1. Conference keynotes
2. New subscriptions campaign success	2. Consolidated vendors through Final Adventure acquisition of Aurasphere	2. Fifteen years of industry experience
3. Team recruitment and development	**3.** Created Channel Partners organization	3. Managed 300 partnerships with distributors
STORY	**STORY**	**STORY**
• **Last Frontier**—Launched subscription package to new and existing consumers, driving historic company growth across three quarters.	• **Vendor Consolidation**—Led the acquisition of three new franchise titles and administered the transition with buyers and retail distributors.	• **Taking a Selfie**—My favorite part of my job is the part I play in bringing consumers' favorite genres to the marketplace. People I don't know come up and ask to take a picture with me...I've never forgotten how it makes me feel. I do it for the gamers!
• **Shrimping Excellence**—Developed my work ethic hauling shrimp on my uncle's boat, where errors meant the loss of the whole catch.	• **Sailing Skills**—Understand the complexities and necessities of teamwork. Sailing requires a team working in tandem to keep a boat moving in the right direction.	
• **Loyalty to the Team**—I know what it means to feel lost. I lost both my parents when I was twenty-two. I've never forgotten those who took care of me, so I make it my mission to take care of people.		• **The Candyman!**—Built conference brand around love of exotic candy. Recognized personality across popular industry conferences.
• **Starting Over**—Moved to California as a lifelong Charleston resident for a fresh start. Had never played a video game, but landed dream job. I know what it's like to have to start over.	• **CPO**—Created a Channel Partners Organization at Big Adventure to ensure smooth partnerships following the Aurasphere acquisition.	• **Keynote**: *Connect Passion to Your Work*—Requested speaker throughout the industry for keynote on Pirate title game that rekindled my love of sailing.

This is defining the experiences within your career story, and you'll notice pretty quickly how much of a differentiator it becomes.

Bernard (Peak Career)

In his peak career phase, Bernard has quite a lot of experience to draw on! In his mapping exercise we learned everything about Bernard, from his love of South American artwork to his scuba diving accident, from his immigrant parents to his show-quality dog. In their peak career, many leaders make the mistake of assuming that people are really only interested in their achievements, that they'll be hired for their next role or given a position on a Board based solely on the results they've achieved. But it's actually the opposite.

While you have acquired a long list of career highlights in your peak-career phase, so have many others. And at this stage, it's even more critical to connect your stories with listeners. Remember the high turnover in the C-suite we discussed back in Section Two? What draws people in and keeps opening new doors is not just your professional experience, but also who you are as a leader and how you position that with an employee base.

Here are the characteristics Bernard might consider:

- *Culture Junkie*: He shifted from law to HR from a passion to grow and support company culture.
- *Patient Coach*: He trained a championship-caliber dog. That takes an incredible amount of patience! He's also had to learn to how manage his later-in-life disability.
- *Community Partner*: He's served on two non-profit Boards to support community health care and early childhood learning centers...because he's been

- inspired by his sister's dedication to education.
- *Diverse Adventurer*: He travels to South America to hunt for artwork and was a frequent scuba diver until his accident.
- *Dedicated Trainer*: He's overseen the training and development of tens of thousands of employees.
- *Purpose-Driven*: In every role he's had since 2000, he's been involved in employee benefits and satisfaction.

As we've mentioned before, the expectations of brand increase throughout your career. And at the peak-career level, so do the expectations of how well you can tell your story. For Bernard, it's not enough just to say he likes helping companies identify and build their culture and that he has a few hobbies on the side. People want to feel connected to their leaders. They don't just want to know that Bernard values company culture, they want to see that culture is the whole impetus behind a major career shift for him. And they don't just want to know that he's an art collector, they want to experience his passion through stories of his annual trips to add to his collection.

Here is Bernard's messaging document:

STATEMENT/GOAL: A veteran HR leader with the desire and experience to help companies execute "people priorities" while delivering employee satisfaction, great customer experiences, and business results.

SKILL SET #1: Servant Leader	SKILL SET #2: Teacher, Coach & Motivator	SKILL SET #3: Culture Junkie
EXAMPLES	**EXAMPLES**	**EXAMPLES**
1. Navigated employees' view through three business transformations	**1.** Global talent strategy that aligns commonalities and differences	**1.** Created a People Priorities playbook leveraged at three companies
2. Peer coaching on harassment and discrimination – from toxic to inclusive	**2.** Developed and launched more than fifteen comprehensive leadership programs	**2.** Built annual plan for reigniting culture feel at two companies – 30–40% lift in customer satisfaction and engagement
3. Overhauled benefits package for flexible and part-time workers	**3.** Designed Corporate University model with online and in-person formats	**3.** Industry-recognized coach
4. Strengthened talent metrics by 50%	**4.** Led and mentored more than forty high-potential cohorts	
STORY	**STORY**	**STORY**
• **YMCA Portland Board**—Led numerous fundraising campaigns for the Portland YMCA. Dedicated to giving back to the community and using fundraising skills to support a non-profit mission.	• **Law to Benefits**—Trained as a lawyer, but saw firsthand how difficult life can be for people without benefits. It stayed with me and changed my career path to get me where I am today.	• **The Coaching Playbook**—Developed playbook for organizational coaching entitled *Own Your Culture, Retain Your People.* Combined decades of experience with how to shift a toxic culture to an award-winning, people-first environment.
• **Experienced HR Leader**—Veteran HR manager with experience navigating organizations through senior-level harassment allegations and toxic work cultures.	• **Dog Show: New Skills**—While training for the Westminster Dog Show, developed my most important skill as a coach: patience.	• **South American Art**—Passionate collector of South American art. Has become an integral part of my philosophy for developing company cultures. Find what you love and find ways to bring it into your work.
• **The High Seas!**—Developed curriculum to support the learning of 1,000+ employees, including onboard learning facilities for our off-duty crew members, while at sea.	• **Learnability & Disability**—Have had to relearn my daily world after becoming partially deaf in mid-life. Has given me a new perspective on the importance of learnability and the ability to relearn and retool.	
	• **Cross-Rotation Cohorts**—Oversaw the launch of a new cross-rotational coaching cohort program, receiving a 96% participant satisfaction score.	

Sharing experiences can turn a communicator from an interviewee or a presenter into an authentic personality. And once you understand what your defining characteristics are and how to develop them into compelling themes for yourself, you're ready for the final stage of building your career narrative: becoming an effective storyteller.

29

Step Three: Bring it to Life

Why do people tell stories?

For thousands of years, storytelling has been the most compelling way to add context to history through generations of people. Stories are the common thread that links us to what has already happened and what is still to come.

And yet, somewhere along the way, we stopped using stories in business settings. And that's where *our* work with storytelling picks up. Because as we've looked at the impact of storytelling in a business setting, we've been hit with a surprising truth: few businesspeople use stories, and they admit to it with some valid excuses.

- Some say storytelling places a higher expectation on a communicator…(it does).
- Some question whether storytelling is appropriate in business…(it is).
- Most say telling stories requires animation and vulnerability…(it does).
- And all say that storytelling has a clear pass/fail feeling with a group…(it can).

But that's where most people miss out on a unique opportunity with a listener. At an individual level, communication comes down to one universal truth: communication occurs when your thoughts connect to the interests and needs of a listener. And there's simply no better way to do that than to tell stories.

In our storytelling workshops and coaching engagements, we teach people how to navigate the art and science of storytelling. We even wrote another book on the topic, *Storylines & Storytelling: What They Remember & Repeat*! For the purpose of your career journey, we'll focus on the structure of stories themselves because it establishes the difference between the description of an event and the impact of a story.

> When I worked at Tumbleweed Farms, Inc., I had a difficult problem with a supplier. Management was frustrated about what they thought was unnecessary overhead and so they sent me out to do a field visit. I was nervous because I was a brand-new hire. It turned out that our entire supply chain issue was caused by one error. It was simple, but it was causing major problems downstream. I've never forgotten that lesson of looking for solutions in simple steps.

That story was told in six sentences. It's succinct and it has a clear point. But those sentences don't help the listener relate to the experience of the storyteller who felt nervous about being sent out to investigate a vendor as a brand-new hire. The example provides context, but it doesn't hit on the key moments an audience listens for. That's why story structure is important. It helps the storyteller think more about what the listener will value in the story rather than just their own accounting of it.

Our story model includes five essential steps:

1. **Set the Stage:** Give the listener some context for the story. What is it about, when and where did it happen, and who are the key players?
2. **Introduce Conflict:** All good stories have conflict or a point at which something has to be resolved. It could be an opportunity instead of a problem. A story needs a reason for something to change, be improved, or be solved.
3. **Solve the Problem:** Once there's an issue or opportunity, the story will logically move toward a solution.
4. **End with Impact:** This is the result of resolving the problem or seizing the opportunity. The impact needs to be significant enough – good or bad – for listeners to feel it was worth their time to get involved in the story.
5. **Wrap It Up:** At the end, the story has to connect back into a conversation or reason why the storyteller shared it.

These five elements transform an example of an event into a story that is memorable to listeners.

Let's go back to Tumbleweed Farms.

I'll never forget the day my boss sent me to Springdale, Arkansas to fire someone. When I worked at Tumbleweed Farms, Inc. I joined a team in turmoil. We were having a difficult time with one of our suppliers, whose every shipment ran three days late and was always twice as expensive as they'd originally quoted us. And my boss had had *enough*! I had been on the team a day and half before he called me into his office and said, "Pack a bag and go tell those morons that either they can get our orders right or I'll find someone who will!"

When I arrived at our supplier's headquarters, I was sweating bullets. I had no idea what I was looking for or how our supply chain worked, yet I'd been sent down there to strong-arm people I'd never even spoken to. Even though I was up all night worrying about the confrontation, I learned quickly when I arrived that their team was as frustrated as our team!

They couldn't understand why we were so angry, as they'd followed our order forms to a T. I spent hours going over every single order from the past year with our account rep and she was right. The orders were correct.

I don't know how it caught my eye, but about three hours in, I glanced at the bottom of the order form and saw the zip code box. Our zip code was off by one number in their system, a two instead of a three.

It turned out our *entire* supply chain was being upended because of a single incorrect number. It was something so simple, yet it had caused countless delays, cost hundreds of thousands of dollars in unnecessary expenses, and it had nearly canceled a long-standing vendor relationship. To this day I've never forgotten "two instead of three" and the lessons that whole experience taught me. Precision matters, and sometimes the most troubling problems are caused by the simplest errors.

As a listener, how did you feel as you read the story? Did you feel the storyteller's nervousness at being thrown into such a heated conflict? Did you feel the manager's anger at his vendor? And did you feel the surprise, relief, and maybe humor in finding out that the cause of so much angst was a single incorrect number? It gets even better when you hear stories told vs. reading them.

Stories don't tell facts as much as they illustrate them. Your listener needs to see a picture, feel the conflict, and become involved in the story. It's about adding the who, what, when, where, and why behind a story. And all of these added elements can be added to a story when it has a clear structure to it.

As you might imagine, it takes a little more time to tell a story and to allow a listener to get vested in the experience, so you can't take up a full interview or an entire presentation telling stories. But you want to be able to leverage a few, because stories are the most memorable elements of any content. We know this because we've measured it. Stories significantly increase how well content is remembered and repeated. And that's an essential skill for an effective communicator.

As you think about your own career narrative, you want to have a bank of stories that you know well and can use to illustrate your brand traits and experiences. As the final step of building the career narrative, we'll take one last look at Victoria, Duncan, and Bernard and show you some examples of what a compelling story to support their career narratives might look like.

Victoria (Early Career)

Stories help bring the literal experiences of your career to life. For Victoria, those themes were *Team Leader, Proven Captain, Creative Explorer, Family-Oriented, Earnest Worker,* and *Global Traveler.* If she wanted to tell a story to illustrate being a diligent worker, it might look something like this:

> There's never a more hectic time at a company than when you're trying to deliver something to a client on a strict deadline...and you run into a problem. During my internship with Premier Global, I was assigned to a project to help construct a financial model that compared pitch stocks across the real estate and energy sectors. My task was to research similar algorithms across the industry to determine best practices and provide analysis for why similar models failed.
>
> The client had a small window of opportunity to beat their competition to the marketplace, and so they stayed closely connected to this project. We had daily check-in calls with the client where we had to keep them up to date on our progress and any potential snags. And the biggest snag we continued to encounter...was on *my* part of the project.
>
> I kept encountering knowledge gaps between our client and the complex data sets that were outside of my expertise. At first, I felt like I was drowning. It was mortifying to have to report each day that I hadn't managed to crack the code yet. I could tell every day that our client was getting antsy about the deadline. I can still hear him clicking his pen repeatedly in frustration!

I probably tried fifty different approaches to building that model, all of which failed spectacularly. I won't bore you with the failed attempts, but think Excel…and more than five hundred pages of analysis that didn't reveal that insights the client needed. It was the fifty-first try that finally worked!

On that project, I learned how to tune out the noise and emotion around a project and focus on solving a problem. I learned the importance of perseverance in the face of seemingly impossible tasks. It might take you fifty-one tries…but you can accomplish great things if you don't get discouraged.

And in fact, our team did accomplish great things. We actually delivered the model a week ahead of schedule.

As a listener, how do you feel about Victoria after that story? Would you agree that she's an earnest worker? How will you feel about her a week later? You might not remember everything discussed in the interview, like what language she's fluent in, what college she attended, or which accounting firm she interned for…but you'll remember that she's a steadfast worker. You'll remember five hundred pages of Excel analysis and that she doesn't give up easily, even if it takes her fifty-one tries to get something right. That's the power of storytelling. It's makes you memorable and repeatable.

Duncan (Mid-Career)

We've learned a lot about Duncan over the last few chapters. Last chapter we learned that his key themes are *Compassionate Leader, Collaborative Partner, Candy Entrepreneur, Consumer Advocate, Convivial Colleague,* and *Skilled Salesman.* For Victoria's example above, she might use that story to impress a recruiter or introduce herself to a new boss. But storytelling is not just an effective tool for interviewing. It's the most effective form of communication to express empathy, impart wisdom, or let a group of people know that they've been heard.

In Duncan's case, he might use his own experiences to create a compassionate story to calm a devastated group of employees:

> I know that many of you are hoping for answers this morning. Harry was our founder, and to lose him in such an unexpected way last month is hard to understand and impossible to accept. We miss our founder and his inspiration, and we worry about what it means for the future of his company and our roles within it. And this morning, I don't know anything more than what you heard last week. I don't have an update from the Board, and I don't know what the company's direction will be.
>
> But I do understand what it's like to feel helpless and worried. Many of you know that my parents adopted me when I was three months old. But you may not know that the year after I graduated college, I lost both my mom and my dad to a car crash.

To say I was devastated doesn't do it justice. My world seemed over, and I couldn't even begin to pick up the pieces. I had lost my support system and didn't know how to think about a new step or even a different path. I felt that way for about a week, and then I got the phone call that changed my life. My best friend from college called me and said, "I know you're hurting right now...but I've got you. I'm here and I will move heaven and earth if you need me to."

I took him up on his offer and moved out West a month later for a fresh start. I slept on his couch for three months and he wouldn't let me pay for a single beer, wash a single dish, or even pick up after his dog. He made my world steady again when I thought there was no way it could ever be put back together. I got my first job in the gaming industry from his couch, and you know the rest of the story. I've been in the industry now for ten years.

My message to all of you today is that all situations get better. I know you're worried and it feels very uncertain right now, but I've got you. I'm here and I will move heaven and earth if you need me to.

We're family here at Aurasphere. Harry always felt that way, and I'm sure we'll find a way to look out for each other in the months ahead.

As Duncan's employee, do you feel taken care of? Even though he can't solve a devastating situation, do you feel like you have a support system you can call on? Did he inspire you to support someone else in the group? Two months from now, will you remember how Duncan made you feel? Duncan's story is a vulnerable one, but it will resonate with a group that's feeling isolated with worry. They'll remember he shared his own vulnerability and made them feel like someone was looking out for them.

Bernard (Peak Career)

In his peak career, Bernard will have a lot of opportunities to share stories. He might tell stories about the company or about himself, about teams he's coached and projects he's led. In the last chapter, we learned that Bernard wants to position himself as a *Culture Junkie, Patient Coach, Community Partner, Diverse Adventurer, Dedicated Trainer,* and *Purpose-Driven.*

With decades of experiences to draw on, Bernard can use these characteristics to speak to almost any group. Here's an example of how he might introduce a new coaching program to employees.

> Learning a new skill is hard, even more so when it means we have to break some bad habits. It's something everyone struggles with…and it's something I was forced to confront about three years ago.
>
> Some of you may know that I love to scuba dive. Every year for the past decade, my family and I have gone scuba diving as part of a family vacation. We've explored reefs in the Caribbean, octopus gardens in the Mediterranean, and my daughter even had an otter swim with me in California. Scuba diving is a beautiful sport, but it can also become dangerous very, very quickly.
>
> I still remember the stingray I was following when I felt a sharp tug on my leg. I turned around, startled to see

my son frantically pointing at my oxygen tank. After all my years of practiced diligence, I had allowed this one stingray to distract me so much that I had lost track of my air. Hurriedly, I kicked my way to the surface, and I came up from too deep too fast.

That dive damaged my right eardrum, which is why today I'm considered legally deaf in my right ear. And at forty-six, the last thing I wanted to do was to learn how to do everything in a different way. Overnight, I couldn't drive, I found it very hard to keep up in meetings, and I felt like I was always three steps behind people, trying to keep up with the conversation.

You've probably noticed that I try to sit on the right side of the room so my left ear can do most of the work. I read lips a lot, and I record a lot of meetings so that I can go back and make sure I don't miss key points. I've learned to cope with my disability, and along the way it's made me a better listener in many ways.

I focus on you when you're talking to me. I take everything in…because I have to, in order to interpret what you're saying to me. My attention is rarely divided or distracted because it takes all of my effort to follow our conversation. And it gives me great satisfaction to hear people describe me as a good listener, because most don't know it's one of the hardest things I do every day.

This coaching program may not be as dramatic as losing partial hearing, but it may be as insightful. It's an opportunity to evaluate habits and rethink how you use your skill set. And I hope you'll allow it to force a different way of considering your opportunities and what drives you and your passion here at Pineapple Software.

As a listener, how do you feel about your CPO? Do you believe that Bernard is committed to helping you find your own passions? Does he seem genuinely excited about this new program? We've talked about the expectations of a senior leader and the ability to motivate and energize employees. It's a combination of personalization and inspiration. You like Bernard not just because he's a good listener, but because he shared the struggle and the personal event that got him there.

As you map your career journey and define the experiences that have shaped who you are, you'll find the stories within you. And as you begin to share your stories, you'll find that people remember them and connect with you because of them.

Whether you're leading a company or just getting started in one, you *can* make an impact by sharing your career experience through stories. We believe in the power of career stories, and that storytelling is a differentiating skill.

And that's a good tie-in to our final phase of this book. Now that we've shown you how we coach someone to build out their career narrative, let's take a look at some success stories of people who were able to use this model to make a compelling pivot in their careers.

30

Career Stories (Early Career)

In someone's early career phase, the term "reset" seems more like a liability rather than an asset at first glance. Recruiters and talent-acquisition teams look at a candidate with too many reset movements in their career as someone who is unsettled and, to a certain extent, unreliable in terms of being a worthwhile investment for a company. Yet as you read in the beginning of this book, talent teams are constantly grappling with what they describe as a lack of top talent, particularly among employees with less than a decade of experience. Which re-raises the question we brought up in Chapter 19: is the talent truly missing, or is it just not promoted properly as part of employees' career narratives?

We've helped early career employees leverage career narratives to:
- Align career direction with multiple career moves
- Transform a skill gap to an applicable job experience
- Connect "disjointed" experiences into an intriguing career path
- Reset personal brand miscues
- Leverage learning moments to highlight development capability

In Section Three, you heard us describe the importance of understanding how to position yourself with a talent team and that theme carried over as we talked through the common mistakes people make in interview settings. Overall, we saw how the inability to connect your brand and your experiences to the functions of a role is what causes a candidate to lose out on a position. And that's a problem that seems to plague early career individuals more than any other group.

Beyond applying and interviewing for their next role, there's a learning curve for young professionals in their ability to blend experiences into a compelling narrative that goes beyond just the mechanical functions or skill sets of their next opportunity. Early career employees are susceptible to being pigeonholed into a particular function with limited experience. You saw this play out in the story from Chapter 17.

And it's easy to see why that happens. Someone with a shorter career history has fewer professional experiences to draw on, which means the absence of a skill is much more apparent than it otherwise might be. If you've been a Marketing Specialist at two companies who specialized in social media advertising, it might be a hard jump for a recruiter to assume that you have the qualifications to be a Global Brand Marketing Manager.

You may not have the experience with email campaign marketing or event management that was a prerequisite for the role, so you have to be prepared to showcase your applicable skill sets and to have a compelling reason why the experiences you have make you an intriguing candidate for the position, particularly if it will cause a talent team to rethink the original scope of a role.

And this remains true within a company as well. Disruption does not just happen from one company to another. As you've seen, disruption happens just as frequently within a company, and as an early career professional, it can be easy to get lost within the corporate shuffle. This is why it's crucial to have an intention behind the brand and career narrative you build. The you that you put forward to an internal team and an internal manager is just as important as the experiences you share for an external role.

Let's look at some examples of intention with resets in an early career.

From Skill Gap to Applicable Experiences

As we built out our three personas in the previous chapters, you saw how we brought an early career narrative to life for Victoria. One of the first roadblocks someone encounters in their career is that 1) their experiences become too uniform (i.e. doing the same specific task at multiple roles), or 2) the opposite, performing apparently "disjointed" functions across multiple companies with no clear path. In either case, it's crucial to know how to leverage the sum of your experiences to paint a clearer picture of what you bring to a role.

And that's what we helped Perry accomplish:
Perry was working as an entry-level Product Engineer at a medium-sized tech company. After a few years, he set his sights on a role at SpearPoint, a prestigious large tech firm

in the Silicon Valley. He'd applied for the role twice, both times making it to the first-round interview before being rejected as "not a good fit" for the position.

After talking through Perry's interview experiences, we discovered that while his resume was solid enough for him to make it into an initial interview, he was struggling to connect his experience in his current role to the expectations of the role at SpearPoint. Perry's experiences on paper painted him as a very functional engineer, but he had a problem: the SpearPoint position called for certification in the Agile process…something Perry did not have. So, when he was questioned about Agile certification, he said "no," and was quickly pigeonholed by SpearPoint's talent team as lacking a specific skill set.

And that's where we were able to help Perry.

In building out his career narrative, we discovered that Perry actually did have proficiency in Agile. In fact, he was probably more skilled than any of the other applicants. His current boss had adopted the Agile format during Perry's first year on the job, and added several modifications and workarounds to it. The boss didn't certify the team because they worked on a custom model, but Perry understood the format inside and out and, even more impressively, he had experience in rolling it and its adaptations out across an organization.

That was the story that Perry needed to tell and it's the one that changed the flow of the conversation. It moved Perry from being someone who did not meet the specific criteria for a role to becoming a leading candidate. And the third time proved to be the charm, as Perry succeeded in landing the position with SpearPoint when he adjusted the way he told his story.

That's our goal when we help candidates think about positioning themselves for new external roles. And our methodology doesn't shift much when we coach someone to position themselves internally.

Internal Upheaval

In your early career, you don't always have visibility to several different managers in an organization. You're placed on a team and you usually work for just one, maybe two, managers. But managers move across a company, and many choose to leave. And in some organizations, that movement feels like a constant churn.

In fact, one of the biggest frustrations we hear from young professionals is that they don't have consistency in managers. They start under one manager, but by the time they have their annual review that manager has moved on. They get disappointed when a promised raise or opportunity falls through the cracks and there's no clear consistency in who is evaluating their work. And when they were close to or had a great working relationship with a manager who suddenly leaves, that pain is even greater.

There's no way to avoid this. It happens every day. But the key to mitigating moving managers is to use that disruption to expand your visibility to other managers.

And it's something Sarah learned to navigate well:

Like many young professionals, Sarah developed a great rhythm with her immediate manager, Frank. She felt like she was firing on all cylinders and was sure to be promoted during her annual review. She knew exactly the position she'd be promoted to and the team she'd be managing. And then the reorg hit.

Frank was reassigned to a different division three weeks before Sarah's review and Sarah didn't know his replacement, Gianna. And this is when we met Sarah. We coached her that, while she couldn't reset the promotion, she did have an opportunity to leverage Frank to expand her network.

When a manager leaves, they know that they're letting their team down. The transition may come at an inopportune time and the team has to adjust to a new manager. So managers who are leaving are generally willing to help you out if you have a specific ask.

Those asks might look like:

- "So Frank, before you leave this role, I'd really like to meet Catherine, who runs our Catalyst product, and I know that you've worked with her a lot. Would you make that introduction for me?"
- "Frank, I would appreciate some honest feedback on what you think I should improve or accomplish over the next six months."
- "Frank, I know you're moving from this team to the Sales Engineering team. I'm really interested in analytics. I'd love to work with you again, if an opportunity presents itself."

Any time a transition occurs internally, a manager will always pass along their impressions and feedback of their team to their successor. Having that conversation with your manager before they leave will give you an opportunity to influence what impressions they pass along.

In Sarah's example, Frank is going to brief Gianna about the team at some point. We coached Sarah to ask Frank for feedback on her work and for advice on her focus for her in the next six months. This will help solidify how Frank represents her and how the new manager develops an initial impression of her.

This is also a great time to clear the air on any misinterpretations of feedback or bad impressions with a departing manager:

"Frank, six months ago, you talked to me a lot about missing deadlines. I really appreciated when you did it, because I did not realize the business impact of a day or two-day delay in my work. But I've really worked hard to make sure that I've delivered on tasks or been ahead of them in the last six months. I want to make sure that you've seen that difference, and that it's no longer an area of worry about me."

This kind of conversation also gives you an opportunity to see what sort of impressions Frank will be passing on to Gianna. If Frank told Sarah that he'd seen her work hard and that he's moved beyond that impression, it's very unlikely that he will share the original incident with Gianna. And if he hasn't seen as much improvement as he would like, now she has given him an opportunity to share that with her before he shares it with Gianna.

Sarah used the opportunity to ask for feedback and asked to stay in touch with Frank, as she was interested in his new team. Frank confirmed that he knew how hard Sarah had been working to overcome the bad impression from delays and that he knew she'd been dealt a bad hand with the reorg. He passed along great feedback to Gianna and Sarah continued the relationship with Frank, checking in with him every few months. Then, eight months later, Frank reached out to offer Sarah a manager position on his new team.

And that's the ultimate goal for early career employees. You want a compelling narrative to be passed around a company. This is the time in your career where you'll experience the most "resets" as you find your footing and build the foundation for a career-long narrative. The determining factor of your success will be your ability to align your experiences to the broader impact of a role.

31

Career Stories (Mid-Career)

Mid-career roles can either be the best positions or the worst ones during companies' fast-paced growth and disruption. As we've mentioned, mid-career is the longest part of most career journeys and many will remain in this phase for the duration of their careers. Storytelling becomes a differentiating tool and skill during this phase, as there is great discretion in who gets visibility as a mid-career manager and who stays nestled within a single department.

We've helped mid-career managers and directors leverage stories to:

- Engage teams in overwhelming projects
- Position themselves as open and personable
- Clarify technical risks to non-technical audiences
- Manage up to simplify details with leaders
- Build credibility and interest with cross-functional groups
- We've also helped them recognize their own challenges and roadblocks with disruption.

Disruption happens at all levels, but for a mid-career leader it can be especially tough because, at many points, experience may not translate cleanly from one company to the next. You may be a senior manager who had been promised a director promotion right before disruption, and may not find it easy to interview for director-level roles because on paper you aren't there yet. Or it could work the other way: you could be titled as a director at one company, while your experience translates to a VP role at the next one. You have to recognize that the journey is a windy road, not a simple trail.

Company disruption puts a mid-career leader in a tricky spot and often reflects on a manager more than they realize when some of the most important decisions are still in flux. Companies shift with mergers and acquisitions, and reorgs and downsizing happen frequently. But once a reorg is announced, a mid-career leader can't help but worry about their own role. And the tricky spot is that their team thinks that mid-career leaders know what's happening, when they really don't. They give insights on valued resources and headcount reductions, but they aren't in the top-level meetings where the decisions are made.

Events like restructures and mergers take time. A lot of time. And it takes senior leadership teams several weeks to build out and communicate their plans as they work through them. Company changes are worked through from the top down in a very methodical way. Tough decisions are made that cause ripple effects that leaders have to think through and deal with before they can move on to the next department.

HR organizations refer to this as "spans and layers." It's the way an organization thinks about talent and resources needed. It's a debate of expense, tenure, and skills. And it involves a small group of senior leaders. But because everyone thinks their manager knows what's going on, it puts an incredible amount of pressure on managers to try and find out.

The most logical step during disruption is to go ask your boss, "Hey, what's going to happen to me? Am I going to be okay?" But in your mid-career you can't act on that impulse, because it sends an immediate signal to a senior leader that your main interest is looking out for yourself.

<u>That's what happened to Jack with his leader, Katie:</u>

A week after an acquisition was announced, Jack was in Katie's office and wanted to know if he would still have a job at the end of the quarter. He wanted to know about his role, about how many resources his team would have to give up, and when the deadline was by which reorg decisions would be made. Katie told Jack to be patient. They hadn't gotten to his department yet, but she knew how hard he and his team had been working and would do all she could to keep the team together. Jack didn't hear her.

It's tough to be patient when you have an entire team worried on the other end. As their leader, you feel like you should be persistent. So, Jack went back to Katie the next week…and the week after. And, picking up on Jack's discontent, his team's productivity began to stall, and many people began quietly looking for other jobs. He lost Katie's trust because she felt like he was putting himself ahead of the company and everyone else. Jack became impatient at a time when mid-career leaders have to illustrate patience and trust.

Katie had been in weekly, sometimes daily, meetings for the upcoming merger, and she had fought hard to try and keep as much of her department intact as possible. And for a while she succeeded. But when the final squeeze came, she had lost a little trust in Jack. She didn't like the qualities she saw when Jack was stressed, and she wasn't sure he exemplified the traits she wanted to see in the leader of her largest team. So she put his peer forward for the role, instead of Jack.

When Katie was forced to make further cuts, it's not surprising that she went with the manager who was cool in a crisis and kept the department moving, rather than the one who fueled the fear of disruption. In times of workplace uncertainty, there *is* always a plan, even if you can't see it yet. And the best advice is patience. Keep the team calm and engaged, even when you don't know what tomorrow will bring. Senior leaders notice who can manage through uncertainty and keep teams focused and moving.

So how do you get in the right column of the resource list? It helps to be a utility player.

Utility Player

We work with more mid-career disruptions than any other phase of the career journey. And that's because it's the biggest group of employees and it's the most critical reset. Mid-career leaders have an interesting view and a tough challenge. They've been in the workplace long enough to know a more methodical pace, so a rapid pace is change. And they didn't start out owning their development path, so the whole process is a reset to them, whether they change companies or not.

And while we see many mid-career leaders displaced and reset, we've noticed one group that seems to be less disrupted than all the others. It's what we call the "utility player." These are the leaders who have found a way to illustrate their thinking and collaboration in different ways. They have high visibility in their organizations, and leaders have begun to value how they think as much as how they work.

Zack was one of those:

We met him when he first moved into a mid-career role, and through a leadership development program, we positioned the idea of visibility and collaboration as brand traits. We talked about establishing a brand of clarity and influence. But we didn't do the work to build those impressions, Zack did. As we watched him progress over a span of five years, we heard about his brand a lot and noticed that he was often added to projects and initiatives as a "utility player." His role on paper was evolving like everyone else's. But his brand was way ahead. He had built value with different teams, and he was a valued opinion on many different initiatives, so much so that leaders knew his story. They considered him an emerging leader in the organization, and when succession plans were discussed, he was always a front-runner. When right-sizing conversations occurred, he always made the right column because leaders know he could be a "utility player" in many different roles. It gave them flexibility to consider him for more than one spot, and that improved his odds every time.

We've watched Zack roll forward through four acquisitions. It's a good position to be in. He didn't get there overnight, but he had a plan for building his brand as someone who brings value in many different ways. He didn't make it hard on others to discover those qualities; he made sure they were visible across the organization. That's an important concept to consider in your mid-career.

It's also important to consider how you tell your story when you are impacted.

Revolving Door

Company ownership can change hands so many times that your resume begins to look more like a game of hopscotch than a clear and intentional career path. But while the buying and selling of a company is something you can't control, you can control the narrative of how that disruption sits within your career.

That's what Laura did, and it made all the difference:

Laura worked as a Senior Director for a mid-sized fintech firm. Within six months of her coming on board, the company was bought, and her role changed slightly. That process brought unexpected speedbumps and challenges, but Laura hung in there and made it through the merger process. Then, after another six months, her company was sold to another large firm. This involved another role change and another round of customer frustration and putting out fires. By the time the company was sold a third time, Laura was a master at managing through disruption.

Until the fourth sale…when Laura's position was eliminated. Despite having helped the company through three mergers in less than two years, she was let go and she was nervous about having to explain to potential employers what she'd been doing for the last two years. Her resume showed three different roles with three different companies, and she didn't want to be seen as a drifter. She was having trouble getting interviews, because her resume didn't tell the full story.

We've met many people like Laura, who view a layoff as a personal failure and something to justify in an interview. But when most people try to justify something they're not proud of, they come across as defensive.

- "I don't understand why I was laid off…I was doing everything they asked."
- "Nobody ever knew what was going to happen next…every day was a fire drill!"
- "It was a terribly run company and, honestly, I was just glad to get out of there."

All of these statements might be true…but they're a recruiter's pet peeve. They don't like to hear negative comments about previous employers. It paints an impression of someone who is jaded or resentful, and that's not a great impression of a potential employee.

But there is a great story in disruption, even if you had to live it to get to it. Remember, talent-acquisition leaders said they were looking for someone who has agility during change and uncertainty. And if you've experienced the revolving door, you have just what they're looking for. You just have to show you thrived in it.

That's what we helped Laura build out in her own career story. She had a unique experience and one that was pretty compelling to a new company. Yes, she might have been laid off due to an acquisition, but she'd also experienced the process three times over and had learned a lot in the process. She had a compelling story as a manager helping a company during its most significant peaks of disruption. And she had the stories to illustrate her ability to lead, adjust, and influence during a transient and prolonged period of disruption. We pulled those qualities forward as we did with Duncan in Chapter 25, and Laura went from feeling defeated to positioning herself as a valued leader. With a reset on her career journey, she was in a new role within six weeks.

Stories of disruption can become memorable sound-bites for a job candidate because they say you adapted to change. Layoffs aren't a black mark against you; they're expected events in a career path. But employers and recruiters listen for how you adapted. Make yours a story about perseverance and adaptability through change. And you'll find that the way you share your journey and your experiences can reset you and your brand beautifully.

Adrienne is one of our favorite stories:

Adrienne was the VP-Engineering at a large tech company. She was employee #16 at the company and she'd been instrumental in helping the company go from small-scale start-up to global name brand awareness. She'd started out sharing a small desk in a co-working space with the Chief Technology Officer, and ended up managing hundreds of engineers all across the globe.

Yet as influential as Adrienne thought she was within the company, that didn't stop her from being disrupted when the C-suite made a sudden change. On Thursday, Adrienne had been looking forward to an annual family beach trip. And then on Friday…things suddenly felt far less certain when her position was eliminated.

But it didn't stay that way for long. Once the layoffs hit the industry press a week later, Adrienne began to get reach-outs from other companies, both from across her professional network and across the industry, who were eager for her expertise. She was interviewing the same week she was let go, and within two more weeks she felt like she was in the driver's seat, with multiple competing offers on the table.

And she would say this was when she realized two things pushed her to the top of the recruiting list: her brand and her story.

Adrienne was a thoughtful and empathetic leader. She was not particularly outgoing or gregarious, but she had built a reputation for high-quality work and taking care of her employees. She often talked at industry events about the value of teams and employees, and people she'd never met often reached out to her about her leadership. She had a following of people who wanted to work for her, and she often hired from those reach-outs.

One company leader reached out to her, saying, "I've never met you, Adrienne, but I used to work with Chuck Dixson at Hourglass Logistics, and he said if I needed a Chief

Engineering Officer that I needed to do whatever I could to hire you. It looks like this may be my opportunity. Would you be available to meet for lunch sometime this week?"

Adrienne also knew how to talk about herself. She wasn't just an engineering leader, she was a *Scalability Specialist.* She'd helped her previous company to scale, and she'd done it twice before that at different companies. She knew how to develop and grow an engineering team. More importantly, she knew how to talk about her experiences in a compelling way.

Adrienne was a team-builder, and she understood the importance of motivation and feeling connected to a greater goal. Every year she volunteered at a local children's shelter, providing games and activities every Saturday. Her signature event was the quilt-making day, where each child was given a square on an enormous quilt to decorate by the end of the day. As children frequently do, many of them would lose interest or get bored halfway through.

Whenever that happened, Adrienne would walk them to the other end of the gym to show them the full quilt being colored in. Without fail, the disinterested kid would re-engage when they saw the full creation coming together. She knew how to empower a sense of accomplishment and ownership.

And that's been a story and approach that Adrienne has shared with many engineering teams. She knows that speed burns people out, but when they are reminded of how their piece of the puzzle fits within an overarching goal, they stay connected and engaged.

Adrienne has become a compelling storyteller, and she uses her own experiences to inspire others. She's embraced disruption because she knows how to reset her brand and her career.

32

Career Stories (Peak Career)

It may be misleading to apply the "reset" term to someone who's headed into a peak-career role. A leader who is on a trajectory to step into a peak-career role doesn't need resetting – it's what they've aimed for all along. And chances are that if they're a candidate for a top position, they've leveraged the concepts you've read about throughout this book. They've got a strong brand and relationships to prove it. And they're ready to position their expertise with key themes of their experience. They'll use stories to illustrate experiences, and they'll be remembered for it.

We've helped peak-career leaders leverage stories to:

- Introduce themselves to a new organization
- Calm uncertainty or change
- Energize a strategy and help groups see the impact of big ideas
- Acknowledge mistakes, struggles, and setbacks
- Humanize and personalize their roles as leaders

This is where storytellers thrive, and it makes all the difference in how their leadership brand is perceived and accepted within a company. The reset for peak careers comes when someone is already in the role or knows they need to step aside in the role. And in both situations, it comes down to always knowing where you stand with your Board, your colleagues, and your employees.

We've helped many top leaders onboard into new roles, and we've seen the difference between those who prioritize relationships and those who prioritize results. It's not an easy choice, but it's an important distinction. Leaders who take the time to understand what they're walking into and to figure out who they can trust set a precedent for relationships. The more you listen, the more you learn. Leaders who feel pressure and urgency to put points on the board often bypass relationships in order to get to quick results. They set the expectation that they will do anything for results, and they often put trust in the wrong people early on. Let's look closer at the power of relationships and a few examples of resetting.

Your Board, Your Peers, and Your Employees

All three are key relationships. If you ask a C-suite leader who their most important audience is, they usually say their employees, and they're right in terms of leading a culture and inspiring a large group toward actions and results. But the other two groups are more important in terms of who defines the leader's success.

Boards hire most C-level roles. They measure success, and they measure impact. But they respond to chemistry.

One of the sound-bites we heard when we talked to an executive search leader was "Leaders get hired for competency, and they get fired over chemistry." We agree. We've seen it multiple times. When a leader ends up sideways with a Board, it never ends well. It always comes down to who knows best, and some leaders just can't stop pushing their agendas. They're usually right in what they're trying to do, but they miss the key to chemistry: it's not about getting it right, it's about bringing others along for the ride. And the urgency to succeed and put points on the board creates a blind spot for leaders.

Peers become critical relationships and a little harder to navigate because they can have competing priorities and competitive personalities. Not all leaders get along. And there can be constant friction to push strategies and ideas through a peer group.

That was certainly the case when we met Barry

Barry was a C-suite leader at a technology company. He was bright, eager, and very driven toward results. He had a peer named Marsha who was also bright, eager, and driven toward results. The problem was that they were never aiming for the *same* result. We heard about these power struggles from Barry's perspective. We suspect Marsha's would have been just the opposite. And over time, we realized that both leaders were investing too much time in the conflict.

We were preparing Barry for a Board meeting where he planned to present a strategy for a new product. It was a great concept and probably a career highlight for him, but he was so consumed with managing Marsha's objections and modifications to it that he got sidetracked in the presentation and didn't do a great job of positioning his idea. Instead, he did a better job of shutting Marsha down.

When we heard his recounts of a bumbled presentation, we knew this wasn't going to end well. So we pushed Barry a bit by asking him, "How does this end?" "Do you see yourself 'winning' over Marsha or do you see yourself working with Marsha to modify the product and get something to market this year?"

His silence spoke volumes. He was in it to win it over Marsha. But leaders never win when companies lose. In this scenario, if you don't see yourself working with Marsha, then you need to rethink your responsibility as a leader. We knew the conflict was on both sides, but the Board and every other peer in the room saw it as Barry resisting Marsha. Overnight, he was on the wrong side of the discussion.

We helped Barry realize that a modified product would be a better company win than his "better" product sitting on a drawing board because two leaders couldn't compromise. All eyes were on Barry to see if he would resolve this. We coached him to go to Marsha and show humility. And we got him there by asking him to think about another time when he was in conflict with a colleague and didn't like the outcome. He had one, and he saw the "win at all costs" comparison.

We nudged him to go to Marsha and admit that he was pushing against her and not pulling ahead for the company. We knew he would need to illustrate that this was a shortcoming of his and that he'd done this before. That's the humility. He shared the previous struggle as an illustration to Marsha that he was trying not to end up there again. He would agree to her ideas and align to them in order to help the company get ahead. And going forward, he wanted to find a way to work with her on common ground instead of stark differences.

We learned later from the CEO that Barry saved his role by working with Marsha. The Board was surprised to see the turnaround and was very pleased by it. Barry told us that it was the hardest thing he'd done as a leader. And Marsha? She shared Barry's story as an example of leadership multiple times within the organization. The power of illustrating intention and humility had an impact on the two leaders and ultimately on the company.

It's Time to Go

Few leaders make this decision voluntarily. They used to, but the shelf-life of a peak-career role is much shorter than it used to be. In Chapter 16, we shared that 17% of publicly traded companies change out their CEOs every year. And as we mentioned in discussing peak-career brands, that kind of frequent change causes similar ripple effects on other senior leaders.

For all the challenges and demands of a peak-career role, there is also a great deal of satisfaction and fulfillment. And it makes it hard to step aside to let the next leader take your place. But it happens, and suddenly you're a peak-career leader with nowhere to go. You got a great severance package, which allows plenty of time to rethink and reset. But most leaders don't want to reset. They'd like to continue to perform in a top role and experience all the stress, pressure, and exhilaration that comes with it. General guidance says you need to reset in a top role within nine months if you want to stay relevant in an industry and as a top leadership consideration.

Not everyone gets that opportunity. Many peak-career professionals find themselves in a position where they don't want to retire yet, but are unsure of what to do next. Some age out of another peak-career opportunity; some price out because their salary and benefits expectations are "too rich" for most companies. Everyone at peak career will reach a point where the next chapter is no longer an upward movement. And plain and simple, this is the time to reinvent yourself and look for something you're passionate about.

It's hard. We've met many leaders at this point who seem a little lost and unsure of how to navigate a next step. Their brand, their success, and their interests are so tied up in that corporate leadership role that it's hard to let it go and reset their direction.

Maggie did that. She recognized that it was time to leave a big corporate job behind, and she looked for opportunities to apply her skills to something very different, from leading a non-profit to joining a young start-up team. But every time she met with a group, the interviewer probably thought, "Wow! You're more qualified than I am to have my job." That's an intimidating presence for a company to take on and most won't because it worries them.

Maggie got frustrated by being overqualified, and that's when we met her. We went back through a few of the opportunities that she had pursued and learned more about the discussions. We discovered that, while Maggie was genuinely interested in the roles, she was presenting her career journey in the same way that she would for a corporate role. We assumed that the opportunities struggled to see how all her experience added value to their team. And we told her that.

In fact, our advice was that in order to get a "smaller" opportunity comfortable with her, she needed to tell less of her story. If she wanted to run the non-profit, it would be more about aligning to their mission instead of telling them how she could triple their contributions through an automated solicitation. If she wanted to work beside the founder of a start-up, she needed to illustrate an interest in learning about the product and its application rather than telling the founder that she had executed four product launches and could do it with her eyes closed. Essentially, we wanted Maggie to share less about herself and focus more on the stories of others.

And we did a pretty radical thing to get her there: we revised her resume to focus on experience and not titles. We took all the corporate labels out other than the experience she gained in each role. Then we worked on upcoming interviews. We built the messaging document, but we shifted the stories. Instead of finding the stories within Maggie, we helped Maggie do the research to find the stories within the organizations.

We knew that the toughest challenge would be getting a group comfortable with Maggie, and she would have to do that for them. When she talked to them, she used their stories to illustrate her understanding and interest in their companies. "Take an interest in me, and I'll take an interest in you" applied again.

Maggie reset beautifully once she understood how to think about her brand and its value to others. She says she's on her "purpose-driven" journey now, and she's having more fun than she ever imagined.

If you choose to continue your journey beyond peak career, you have to reset the narrative. Few top leaders reset on past experiences. They do it best by resetting on what they want to do and illustrating a willingness and desire to keep learning and growing. It may not always be well-timed, but as long as you're willing to repackage your story, it may be the most rewarding chapter of your career.

33

Bringing Brand and Stories Together

As the book comes to a close, we hope you're confident about the tools it takes to turn disruption into success. Because while disruption has presented a whole new outlook for careers, the truth is, it has also introduced more opportunity into the workforce than ever before. You just have to know how to seize the opportunities.

Disruption *will* happen. It's as inevitable as the flow of time, and many times it's the result of circumstances outside of our control. And while disruption might be just that, *disruptive*, to our day-to-day lives and our professional careers, the key to resetting yourself and turning disruption into opportunity comes from having a memorable brand and a compelling career story.

As you think through your own reset, keep these takeaways in mind.

You are responsible for managing your own career and development. Relying solely on others to advance your career makes any promotion or expanded visibility a matter of timing, rather than of fit or ability. If you want to seize opportunities, you have to take ownership for your development and be intentional about the skills you have and those you need to learn.

You need to understand your brand, your skills, and how both fit in your journey. The first step toward building a brand and a narrative is to understand how others think of you. Ask for feedback, make sure you understand the feedback, and then use those discussions as a benchmark to measure your ability to shift and strengthen impressions.

A career path doesn't follow the traditional model of career advancement. There's no printed guide map of what success looks like. There are set expectations that you can 1) think critically 2) collaborate and communicate effectively and 3) adapt to periods of change and uncertainty. Learn how to turn your experiences into a compelling case for how you meet those expectations in a role.

Someone who shapes their career will have more options than someone who does not. Companies *want* employees with unique backgrounds. An interview is less about what you can do and more about how well you align your experiences to a company's goals. Positioning yourself is not always about proving you're the smartest person in the room. But it *is* always about proving that you have a compelling perspective that can solve a need.

Transferable skills and talents transcend job functions. Your skill set may not always line up perfectly with what someone thinks they're looking for in a role, but people are willing to be convinced.

That's why high-profile companies have hired:

- A Head Chef to be a Director of Customer Service...because they've mastered customer satisfaction, attention to detail, management, and high-pressure environments.
- A Radio DJ to be a Sales Manager... because they know how to talk to people from all different walks of life and are experts at connecting with people they can't even see.
- Or a Zookeeper to run Supply Chain Logistics... because they understand the importance of maintaining a steady supply flow for a variety of unique and complex clients.

The proof is in the stories that we've shared and the ones that are still to come. Let's take a final look at how Adrienne, the engineering lead in Chapter 31, experienced it.

Adrienne was the quiltmaker, and she brought the same approach she used with her volunteer experiences to her engineering teams. She understood that speed burns people out. But when they have a line of sight to how their piece of the puzzle fits within an overarching goal, they'll stay connected and engaged.

That's how Adrienne talked about herself...and people remembered it! In fact, after telling her quilt story in an initial interview, Adrienne came into the final panel round with leaders she hadn't met yet and the CEO jumped up and exclaimed, "It's the quiltmaker!"

That's where we hope your career and your stories are headed: from a place of working hard on your brand and your journey, to a place where your brand and your journey are working hard for you. Because when you've built a captivating narrative, you'll find that it draws people to you. And in a world of career disruption, the most marketable and dynamic skill set you can have is a brand and a story so compelling that others are waiting in the wings to snatch you up.

No matter where you find yourself in your career, we believe it's always possible to hit reset. There are endless opportunities ahead…so here's to defining your own success!

Disrupted!
Appendix

Talent Development Survey

180 Talent Development Leaders who work in various industries including Technology, Healthcare, Hospitality, Retail, Manufacturing & Logistics

92%   Mid to Senior Level

73%   Have more than 10 years experience

60%   Work for large enterprises

Talent Development's Highest Priorities

*Which level or position is the **highest priority** within your company today?*

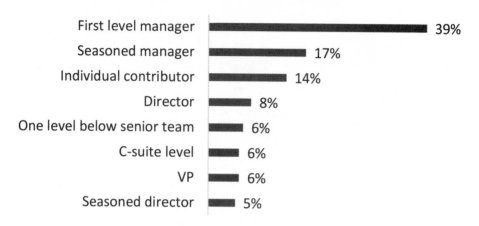

First level manager	39%
Seasoned manager	17%
Individual contributor	14%
Director	8%
One level below senior team	6%
C-suite level	6%
VP	6%
Seasoned director	5%

Why is this group a priority?

New business objectives, goals, and initiatives	24%
Young leaders who need leadership skills	19%
Want to get them ready for leadership early	16%
Lack specific skills	11%
They are new people managers	10%
Trying to retain them	7%

Skilled first-level managers are needed to help organizations achieve goals. According to empirical research, often, the first-level manager has a lot of visibility and needs to have specific skills because they work directly with customers & employees. Also, they influence employees to achieve business goals.

Talent Development's Lowest Priorities

Which level or position is the **lowest priority** within your company today?

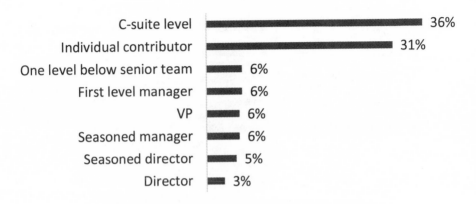

C-suite level	36%
Individual contributor	31%
One level below senior team	6%
First level manager	6%
VP	6%
Seasoned manager	6%
Seasoned director	5%
Director	3%

Why is this group the lowest priority?

Well-qualified for their current roles	51%
Other (see below)	24%
Unsure	19%
We expect turnover at this level	3%
Was a priority last year	3%
Overqualified for their current roles	0%

Other:
- It is not in the budget
- Need buy-in from leaders
- Limited resources
- We have long-tenured senior managers with solid skills that need refreshing
- We develop leaders to develop individual contributors
- This group does not think they need training

Talent Development: Top Challenges

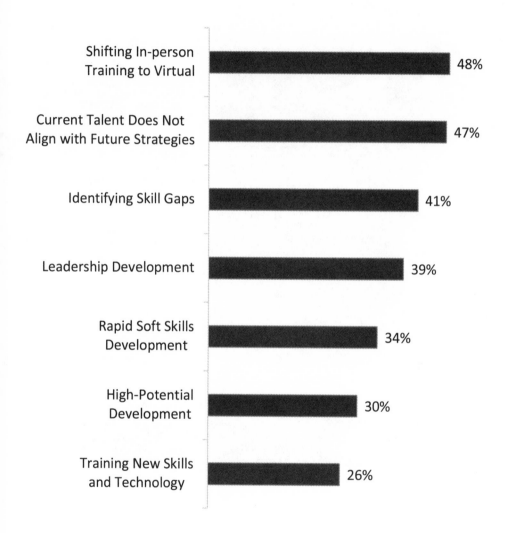

Talent Development:
Company & Employee Goals

PRIORITIES

82% of talent development priorities are based on company goals, identified gaps (to do specific tasks), and job roles & functions.

PRIORITIES

8% of talent development activities are based employee feedback and development interests.

Talent Development: Critical Skills

What skills are most needed in your organization?

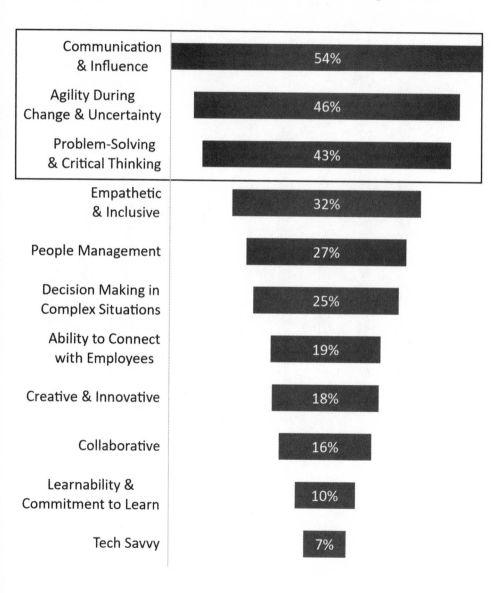

Skill	Percentage
Communication & Influence	54%
Agility During Change & Uncertainty	46%
Problem-Solving & Critical Thinking	43%
Empathetic & Inclusive	32%
People Management	27%
Decision Making in Complex Situations	25%
Ability to Connect with Employees	19%
Creative & Innovative	18%
Collaborative	16%
Learnability & Commitment to Learn	10%
Tech Savvy	7%

Talent Development:
Training Investment
Department & Function

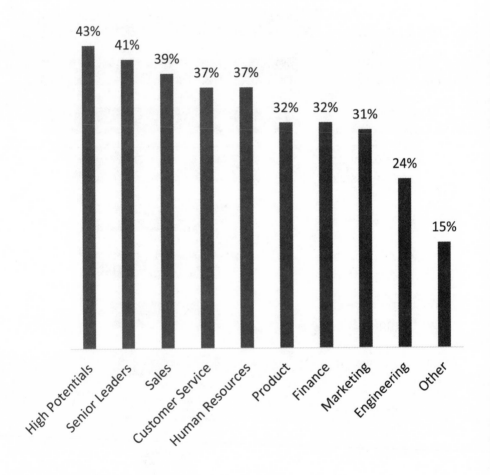

Employees Across All Functions Ask For:

MANAGEMENT SKILLS

LEADERSHIP SKILLS

COMMUNICATION SKILLS

TECHNICAL SKILLS

Talent Development: Additional Insights

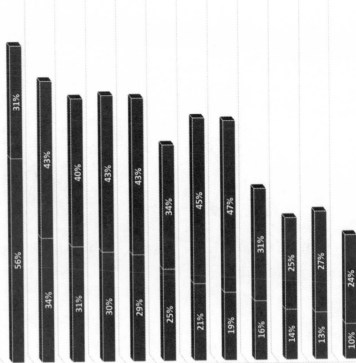

Legend: ■ Strongly agree ■ Agree

Statement	Strongly agree	Agree
Individuals should understand how their brand and skills fit in their career.	56%	31%
Career paths don't follow the traditional model of career advancement.	34%	43%
People are responsible for managing their careers and development.	31%	40%
Skill development motivates employees to stay with an organization.	30%	43%
Employees should seek skills beyond their job to advance their career.	29%	43%
My organization promotes training and development opportunities.	25%	34%
An individual should take calculated risks in their career.	21%	45%
Individuals must position themselves for career advancement.	19%	47%
In my organization, employee development is a priority.	16%	31%
My organization helps employees reach their career goals.	14%	25%
My organization takes a personal interest in employees' career goals.	13%	27%
Your current job is the best way to get skills to advance your career.	10%	24%

Talent Acquisition Survey

100 Talent Development Leaders who work in various industries including Technology, Healthcare, Hospitality, Retail, Manufacturing & Logistics

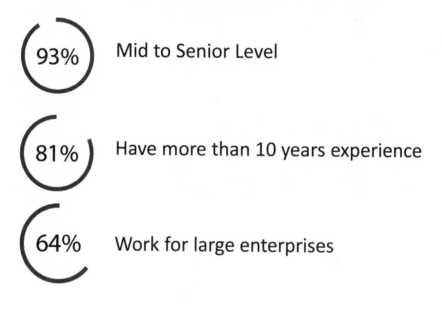

93%   Mid to Senior Level

81%   Have more than 10 years experience

64%   Work for large enterprises

Talent Acquisition: Top Challenges
Identifying & Acquiring Highly Qualified Talent

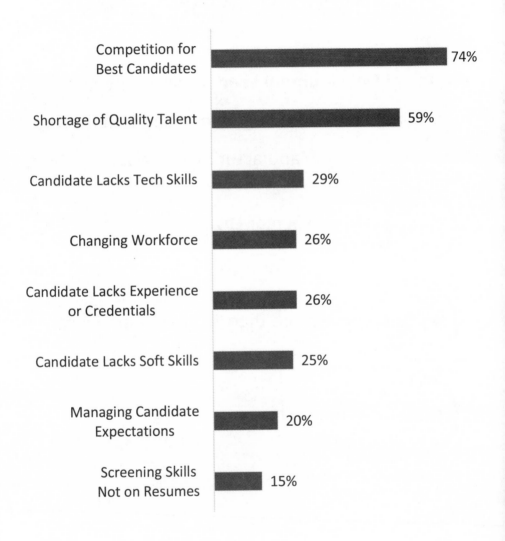

Talent Acquisition: Critical Skills

What skills are most needed in your organization?

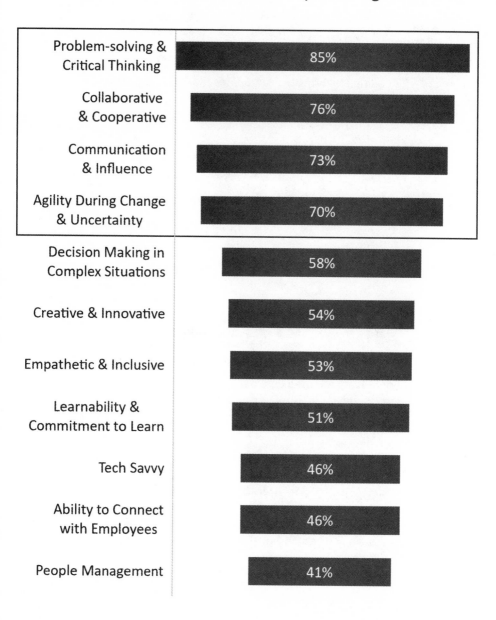

Talent Acquisition: Top Goals

100%

Acquiring high-quality candidates that offer critical skills needed for current available roles.

91%

Building a diverse talent pool to meet current and future business needs.

83%

Identifying talented employees within the company to groom for promotion.

83%

Assessing current in-house skills to determine future skills and roles needed.

Talent Acquisition: External vs. Internal

Reason for Selecting External Talent vs Internal

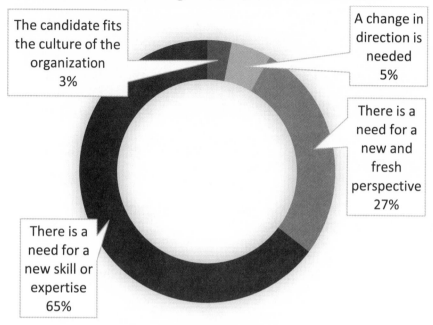

The candidate fits the culture of the organization
3%

A change in direction is needed
5%

There is a need for a new and fresh perspective
27%

There is a need for a new skill or expertise
65%

Reason for Selecting Internal Talent vs. External

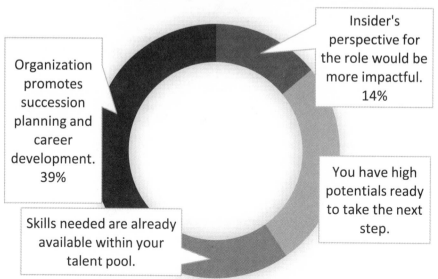

Insider's perspective for the role would be more impactful.
14%

Organization promotes succession planning and career development.
39%

You have high potentials ready to take the next step.

Skills needed are already available within your talent pool.

Talent Acquisition: Interviews

What Makes a Candidate Memorable?

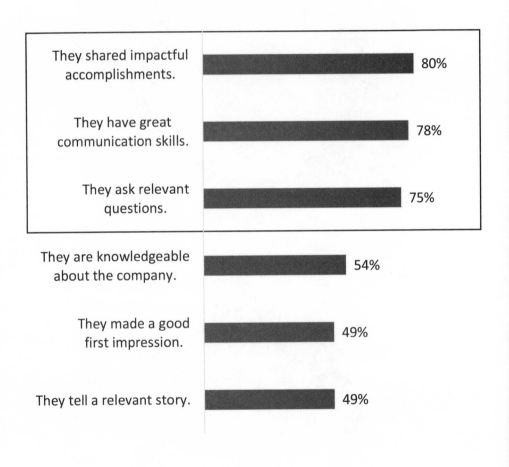

They shared impactful accomplishments. — 80%

They have great communication skills. — 78%

They ask relevant questions. — 75%

They are knowledgeable about the company. — 54%

They made a good first impression. — 49%

They tell a relevant story. — 49%

Talent Acquisition:
Body Language & Physical Appearance

Virtual & In-Person Interviews

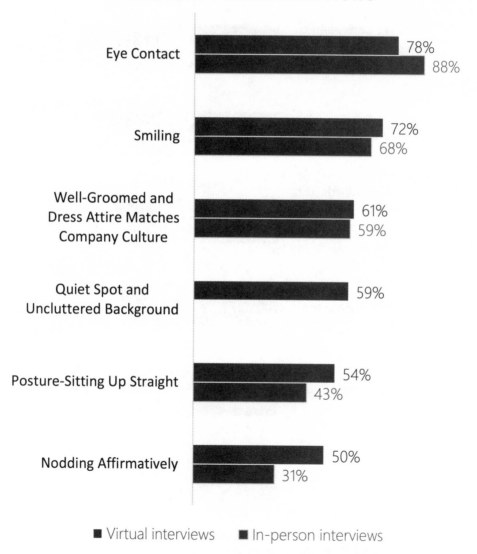

Talent Acquisition:
Voice Delivery & Verbal Cues

Virtual and In-Person Interviews

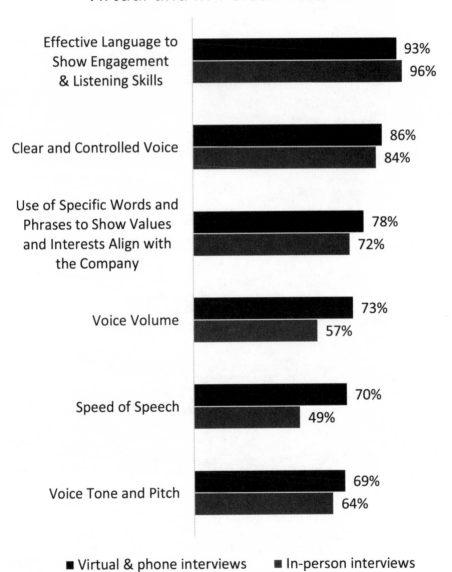

Effective Language to Show Engagement & Listening Skills: 93%, 96%

Clear and Controlled Voice: 86%, 84%

Use of Specific Words and Phrases to Show Values and Interests Align with the Company: 78%, 72%

Voice Volume: 73%, 57%

Speed of Speech: 70%, 49%

Voice Tone and Pitch: 69%, 64%

■ Virtual & phone interviews　　■ In-person interviews

Talent Acquisition:
Interviewing Blind spots

Candidates:

- Are not prepared. They don't have a resume; they don't know the company and they don't know the interviewer.

- Can't answer questions relevant to the position.

- Don't ask questions relevant to the position.

- Don't answer questions succinctly. They ramble and often don't seem to have a solid answer.

- Don't always show up professionally in terms appearance and attire and interaction with others in an office.

- Share negative opinions of previous employers which reflects poorly on the candidate.

- Don't take online interviews seriously and are often too casual in their approach.

- Don't connect well with interviewer and seem unaware of how body language impacts the interview (online and in-person).

- Don't prepare for setting of virtual interviews, in terms of technology and non-distracting environment.

Talent Acquisition: Additional Insights

■ Strongly Agree   ■ Agree

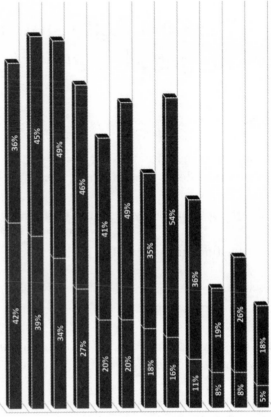

Statement	Strongly Agree	Agree
Individuals who shape their careers may have more options than others.	42%	36%
Individuals should understand how their brand and skills fit in their career.	39%	45%
Online profiles are important to personal brand and impressions.	34%	49%
People are responsible for managing their careers and development.	27%	46%
My organization leverages technology to recruit and segment talent.	20%	41%
Individuals must position themselves for career advancement.	20%	49%
Transferable skills hold more weight than academics and work experience.	18%	35%
Transferable skills and talents transcend industry or job function.	16%	54%
Internal mobility and succession planning are used to harness employee skills.	11%	36%
It is challenging to identify candidates for skills required in my organization.	8%	19%
My organization pulls from a developed talent pool to fill a position.	8%	26%
My organization has a clear plan for career growth to retain employees.	5%	18%

Talent Acquisition vs. Talent Development: Top Critical Skills

TALENT ACQUISITION

1. Problem-solving & Critical thinking

2. Collaborative & Cooperative

3. Communication & Influence

TALENT DEVELOPMENT

1. Communication & Influence

2. Agility during change & uncertainty

3. Problem-solving & Critical thinking

Talent Acquisition vs Talent Development: Critical Skills

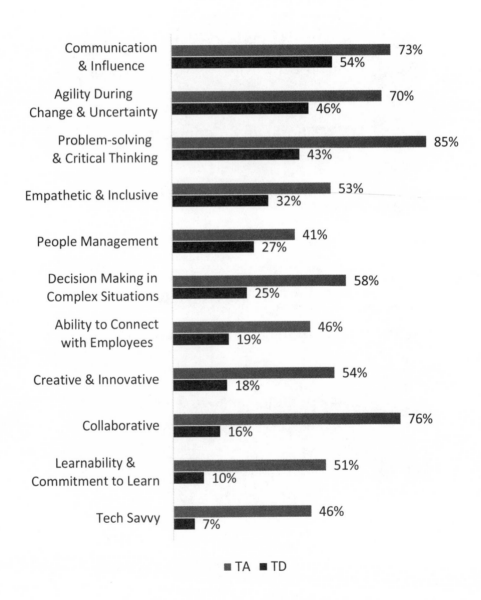

Disrupted! Resources

MY PERSONAL BRAND

Strategic-thinker Detail-Oriented Results-oriented focused
PERSUASIVE Motivating authentic COMMANDING
Confident PROMOTER ETHICAL driven
contributor INFLUENTIAL supportive pessimistic SELF-STARTER
Decision-maker reliable committed
Communicator Compelling
complex supportive contextual friendly Successful
concise Integrity task-oriented
caring FLEXIBLE Impactful Leader honest
LITERAL teacher CONVINCING Responsible Artistic
Critical-thinker DECISION-MAKER Planner engaging High potential

Your brand is like a trademark that combines all the elements of you into someone else's experience of you.

PART I: Impressions – What You Think
List six attributes that you believe best describe you.

1. _____   4. _____

2. _____   5. _____

3. _____   6. _____

PART II: Impressions – What Others Think
List attributes that you think others would describe of you next to each statement.

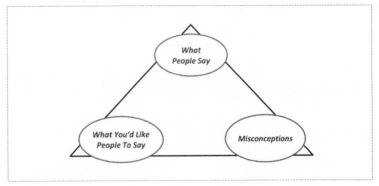

MESSAGING DOCUMENT: EXAMPLE

STATEMENT/GOAL: This is where you write your goal that the following skills will support.

SKILL SET #1: Skill 1

EXAMPLES
1. Skill set example 1
2. Skill set example 2
3. Skill set example 3

STORY

- **Supporting Story 1**

SKILL SET #2: Skill 2

EXAMPLES
1. Skill set example 1
2. Skill set example 2
3. Skill set example 3

STORY

- **Supporting Story 2**

SKILL SET #3: Skill 3

EXAMPLES
1. Skill set example 1
2. Skill set example 2
3. Skill set example 3

STORY

- **Supporting story 3**

Stories help audiences understand our ideas. Storytelling is the most effective way to help someone relate to information and consider its impact on them and others.

Stories that are based on experiences can help a listener relate to a specific character or event and understand what you're asking them to do. To tell a good story, make sure there is a main character in the story and that you embellish the core elements of the story with color commentary or details that help us hold onto specifics such as location, time of day, identifiable people and places that tie the story to the audience. Listeners will hold onto memorable anecdotes within your story which helps them remember it and repeat it after they hear it.

Build the Experience Story

1

Set the Stage.
Start with context that helps the audience imagine the situation.

2

Introduce the Point of Conflict.
You want your audience to relate to the main character and to see themselves as the person you are describing.

3

Solve the Problem.
Tell how the conflict is resolved.

4

End with Impact.
Whether the story has a happy ending or a surprise ending, it needs to have impact.

5

Wrap Up.
Tie the ending back to the concept/message you wanted to introduce.

EXERCISE: BUILD YOUR EXPERIENCE STORY

Use the framework provided to map out the elements of your story.

1. **Set the Stage.** *Start with context that helps the audience imagine the situation.*

   _____

   _____

   _____

   _____

2. **Introduce the Point of Conflict.** *You want your audience to relate to the main character and to see themselves as the person you are describing.*

   _____

   _____

   _____

   _____

3. **Solve the Problem.** *Tell how the conflict is resolved.*

   _____

   _____

   _____

   _____

4. **End with Impact.** *Whether the story has a happy or a surprise ending, it needs to have impact.*

   _____

   _____

   _____

   _____

5. **Wrap Up.** *Tie the ending back to the concept/message you wanted to introduce.*

   _____

   _____

   _____

About Sally Williamson & Associates (SW&A)

Sally Williamson & Associates is a trusted resource for developing leaders worldwide. For more than three decades, the firm has coached C-level executives, mid-level managers and high-potential employees on the impact of brand and the ability to influence through communication.

And it all started with the vision and passion of Sally Williamson, the firm's founder and expert in all things related to spoken communication. Sally brings more than three decades of experience, insights and a general love of connection to empower more than 15,000 leaders and managers to influence and impact any group. But she's most proud of the team she's built that helped us grow from the passion of one to the power of many. And that's why her fourth book includes two colleagues who bring their own unique powers.

Hurst Williamson is our ultimate utility player who can uncover client needs, lead a workshop or weave an incredible tale. He owns every room and brings genuine engagement to communication. He is the heart of the career journey and a proud member of the generation most disrupted. But he sees it as an opportunity to tell your story and own your journey. And he's helping many of our clients do just that.

LaKesha Edwards is a life-long learner who loves research, insights and discovery. With a PhD added to her own career journey, she questions what we're learning and how we're solving it. And with SW&A, she creates the steps to continue a development experience by thinking through what we learn, what we teach and how we coach. And quite frankly, she keeps us all on our toes.

For more information about Disrupted! and SW&A's services, visit www.sallywilliamson.com